FRAGILE CREATURES

KHIN MYINT

FRAGILE CREATURES

A MEMOIR

Published by Black Inc., an imprint of Schwartz Books Pty Ltd
Wurundjeri Country
22–24 Northumberland Street
Collingwood VIC 3066, Australia
enquiries@blackincbooks.com
www.blackincbooks.com

9781760645144 (paperback)
9781743823620 (ebook)

A catalogue record for this
book is available from the
National Library of Australia

Cover design by Akiko Chan
Text design by Beau Lowenstern
Typesetting by Tristan Main
Cover image courtesy of the author

Author's Note

This is a work of narrative non-fiction. It's based on subjective memory, like all memoirs. It is as honest as I am capable of making it. I have changed most names, including those of Rachel and her family. My own family's names remain intact, as do those of public figures. I am grateful to have a family, small as we are, who have given me their blessing to publish this. This memoir is dedicated to them.

Part One

One

I ashed my cigarette and watched the pale ribbon rise below a June-blue sky. Mum picked at the other couch's armrest and looked at me.

'All I know,' she said, 'is that your sister didn't ask me.'

She sighed and I took another drag. My sister had lived the last thirteen years with our mother in this duplex, and since shifting back here myself last week, I'd spent most of my time on these outside couches.

'It's good that she has to ask someone before she can get to it,' I said.

Mum nodded.

The thing we were talking about was a key that opened a box my sister was keeping under her bed. Inside was a drug called Nembutal that she'd ordered from a Mexican website. It had arrived a week earlier and Theda had given the key to her boyfriend, Samuel. The arrangement meant she would need to call him before accessing it, which was wise since my sister didn't want to die. She just wanted an escape hatch nearby. She said it was easier to keep going, knowing that a painless way out was within reach.

The search for treatments for her had led everywhere from neurologists to psychiatrists to psychics. Her illness was not fatal but seemed incurable, and its cause was unknown. Or, perhaps more accurately, its cause was debated. Theda was suffering, but experts disagreed on why, and her right to sympathy hinged on the cause. If it was physical, she got compassion, exemptions and affordable treatments. But if her condition was mental, she was a *hysteric*.

Conversion disorder was the contemporary term for hysteria, and Theda had grappled with some doctors giving her that diagnosis, along with ones who adamantly told her it was something else. For a while, some doctors had said my sister had chronic fatigue syndrome. This had lasted ten years. A new doctor had shifted her diagnosis to chronic Lyme disease in the last three.

As for me, I was uncertain, but it worried me that the psychiatrists who said she had conversion disorder might be right. If they were, then the cause most likely came from our childhood. The racism we'd both experienced growing up hadn't been easy but we'd also been torn between two parents from different cultures – one white and Western, one Eastern. Our father resented the white parts of us and had berated us for them growing up, whereas our mother had encouraged us to be Western and the kids at school had bullied us for being too Asian. I had always suspected my sister's illness was tied to our childhood troubles. But she and my mother disagreed, so I never said anything about it anymore.

Theda was thirty-seven and couldn't watch TV or use a computer. She barely ate any foods beyond the blandest ones I could imagine. She suffered migraines and nerve pain. She was so fatigued that all she did was lie in bed. And a few years ago, she had asked Mum and me for permission to die. We'd both given it, in our ways – Mum more directly than me – but the reality was much harder to comprehend now that the Nembutal was here.

I glanced over at Mum. She looked pensive. Abstract thinking had never been her forte, but she was pragmatic and strong. She'd raised me with a working-class version of feminism that was deeply compassionate.

'What about you?' she said.

I eyed my cigarette.

'Will you quit those?'

'Soon,' I said.

'Any word from Rachel?'

I shook my head.

'How could anyone change their mind so quickly?' She looked at me for a moment longer, then slowly got up, leaving me on the front porch to my cigarettes and the June weather.

★

Eighteen months earlier, while doing aid work in Thailand, I had met an American woman. When we met, I was thirty-four, and she was twenty-four. We fell in love and returned to Perth. The plan was to stay for a year but ultimately move to the US and get married. After a year in Australia, she said she wanted another year, so we began applying for an Australian de facto visa that would allow her to keep working. The application documents were in a lever-arch file on our coffee table, ready to go. But a few days before it was due, she changed her mind and flew back to her mother's house in Albany, New York.

Rachel's childhood had been different to mine, and perhaps for that reason I didn't fully comprehend her reasoning, but it had something to do with ambition and my inability to lubricate hers. Her mother, Mary Devison, had visited us four months before Rachel's turn and made her feelings clear: I wasn't good enough for her daughter's future.

I remembered bringing Mary tea after her long flight from New York to Perth. She was a bespectacled blonde woman in her fifties with a slight hunch. Her suitcase was still unopened in the corner of our lounge room, and I had three cups and some biscuits on a tray. Rachel asked her how the family dog was going.

'Oh honey,' Mary said, scrunching up her face. 'Oh, darling. Oh, he was—' She looked up at me as I approached, holding the tray. 'It was just so … important that I come and talk to you about these …' – she looked at me again and then at her daughter – 'these *decisions* you're making.

'He needed so much care, and no one could look after him. Your brother has college, and your father … well, you know … his job is high stress. It was too important that I come and talk to you about—' She glanced at me again. 'When I see you making mistakes … Honey, I put him down.'

In bed that night, Rachel cried. 'I did warn you,' she said. 'She's a bit nuts.'

'She killed the dog,' I said, trying to make sense of it, 'because she wanted to come and talk you out of marrying me?'

Rachel looked at me with troubled eyes. 'He was getting old anyway,' she said.

I breathed a sigh of relief when it was time for Mary to leave.

'She commanded me home,' Rachel said at the airport, after her mother had passed through the gate. 'While you were in the toilet, she said to me, "Rachel, I am your mother, and I command you to come home right now."'

I didn't want to cause trouble, so I shrugged it off. Rachel had told me not to worry about her mother. She was going to marry me no matter what, and her mother didn't control her. I'd taken that at face value, and it never occurred to me that I was already in battle and needed to fight.

For the next two months, Rachel and I talked about her grad school plans for the following year, when we planned on returning to her country. We talked about what we might name our children one day and which small towns in America we might move to. Her anxiety flared up, but she told me it wasn't a big deal and I encouraged her to take medication if that helped. She was happy otherwise, and I figured it wasn't anything major. She said she was delighted with everything in our lives and didn't really know why she was anxious, but that sometimes it just happened.

And then, eight weeks ago, she left me.

She'd not been very aware of whatever was going on either, because a week before that, she had taken my mother out for lunch to discuss wedding plans. I'd spoken to Mum on the phone afterwards and she'd talked about how excited Rachel was. I think Rachel didn't know she was leaving me until a day before she did. The week before, she'd asked me to start organising a party to announce our engagement to friends. A few days before she left me, she had put Post-it! notes around the apartment, stuck to the insides of cupboards, with little messages saying things like, *I love you, Khindle. I can't wait to spend the rest of my life with you. I never thought I'd be so lucky.* She was like that – prone to cute acts of loving expression that were childlike – and I appreciated it. I was the same.

Then she was gone.

We spoke on Skype once she was back in America. Her reasons seemed thin and hastily assembled, as though she was trying to string together a clearer explanation in her own mind too.

'I was hiding my mental health problems,' she said. 'I panicked. Mom was sending emails telling me I was ruining my life. It just got too much, worrying about whether she was right.'

'Can we save us?'

'Yes,' she said. 'Come here, and we can sort it out. It'll be like we planned. Just a year early.'

I should have gone straightaway, but I felt obligated to finish the semester's teaching. My family needed time for me to say goodbye, and I had to get rid of the apartment I was renting. It took four weeks, and we spoke on Skype every day. Rachel seemed fine, and I was careful not to rock the boat. I wanted to talk about what had happened to make her leave so unexpectedly but figured we might have better conversations in person. Then, a week ago, she changed her mind again.

'What do you mean?' I said over Skype, after she had announced it.

'In my field,' she said, 'in *social justice,* I can't have this *amazing* career if I'm married to someone like you. I just can't.'

'Why not?'

'You don't earn enough money, Khin. You're an English second language teacher and that might be enough in Australia but here it won't work. I want a baby one day, and a career in this really competitive industry. Social justice work is hard to get – you know that. When we have kids, I'll need you to support me for a while. I don't think you'll be able to do it.'

'But we always talked about raising children like a modern couple,' I said.

'That's not realistic, Khin. My mother has been alive longer than either of us and talked to me about it really seriously. I get that it's upsetting, but we have to face reality.'

'Did your mother—'

'My mother *knows* me, Khin,' she snapped. 'We went to a dance performance together last night and it just … it was … it was *awesome*, Khindle. You should have—' She hesitated at the irony. I could see her getting excited via our Skype connection as she remembered. It was as if she was manic. 'They were at the top of their field, Khin, from *New York City*. It's just … things are so different here. I'm more myself now – and the way their bodies were extensions of their minds … it … I can't explain. It was just—' She paused, still searching for words to describe this dance performance's importance.

'Mom was talking to me in the theatre bar afterwards and I realised that I could be just like those dancers, in my way, in social justice, but not if I marry you, because you're going to hold me back, Khindle. You really are. I'm very sorry. I still love you, but I need to do this.'

'I'll come,' I said. 'So we can talk in person.'

I can't explain what happened next. I witnessed it, but it didn't make sense to me. Her mood suddenly switched, and she began screaming inchoately. Spittle was coming out of her mouth and landing on the webcam. She was imploring me not to come, but more than that, she was also insulting me and swearing, calling me names and saying I was threatening her. *'Just be a man, Khin,'* she yelled amid a tirade of other jumbled and confusing phrases. *'Just be a fucking man!'*

That was the week my sister's euthanasia drug arrived. I had no job and nowhere to go. So I took up smoking again – an old habit – and accepted Mum's offer to move home.

★

I put out my cigarette and went inside, where I saw Mum was in the kitchen. I slipped quietly down the hallway to my sister's door and knocked.

'Come in?' she whispered.

When I opened the door, her room was dark and cool. Opaque curtains covered the window, and the only light was a soft blue glow coming from an air filter that made silhouettes out of the furniture. Photo frames on the bookcase held images I couldn't quite make out. Mum had been given money for a humidity-controlling air conditioner a couple of years back, so the climate inside hadn't changed since I'd last entered.

'Sorry,' I said.

'What for?'

'I've been smoking. I stink.'

'It's okay,' she said patting the bedclothes. 'Do you want to listen to my audiobook?'

Her figure on the bed was slender and fragile. Once she'd been vivacious; now she was withered like an old lady. We hugged and I retired to the armchair near the bottom of her bed. She often just wanted company rather than conversation. If talking was too tiring, we usually listened to a story. This one sounded somewhere in its middle, about an intergalactic space-travelling race searching for a new home.

I sensed Theda settling back down, and my thoughts returned to Rachel. The audiobook narrator droned in the background as I thought of how Rachel had said something about wanting a rougher lover.

We'd talked again after she'd calmed down following the last call, when she told me to be a fucking man. She spoke again about my masculinity and how it was more incompatible with her desires than I'd ever imagined. She talked about wanting a much more dominant guy in the bedroom. I'd thought our sex life was good until then. She'd always come during sex until the last couple of months when her medication had made it difficult.

She also told me that I didn't believe in her, which made no sense to me. 'What do you mean?' I said.

'Someone who sees my true potential wouldn't have let me stay in Australia when it was wrong for me,' she said.

When I reminded her that she'd been the one wanting to stay an extra year in Australia, she shifted gears again. 'Someone right would know what I need. Someone right for me would have seen I needed to go back to America, even if I couldn't see that myself.'

I couldn't understand the reversals and suspected she didn't know why she'd ended things. 'The world isn't like we imagined, Khin,' she said eventually. 'Maybe in Australia it is. But the American world isn't like that.'

Theda's audiobook stopped playing and my mind tumbled back into the present. I looked up to see my sister staring at me over her bed-clothes. 'I'm sorry,' I said. 'You must be able to feel my heavy thoughts?'

'Don't be silly.' She turned the audiobook back on and we listened for a while longer before she said she wanted to rest alone.

★

The next day, I sat on the porch pondering what I should do now that Perth was my only future again. I had been imagining America for the last two years. Before meeting Rachel, ending up as my sister's full-time carer had been a looming crisis. It wasn't a future I wanted, least of all because I knew it would entail conflict about her diagnosis. Mum was seventy now and would deteriorate, and when I was left in charge I would probably push for mental health treatments and Theda would see it as a betrayal. She'd hate me for it, but what choice would I have? This was a future I'd thought I could avoid, and which had worried me immensely before Rachel. Now it wasn't just about Rachel being gone; it was about what that did to my escape-from-Perth plan. The idea of staying in this godforsaken city didn't seem like a future. I didn't believe I'd ever meet anyone I could connect with here.

Somewhere among these thoughts, I started to google Rachel's anti-anxiety medication. She'd only started taking it a couple of months ago and I was wondering about it. Since leaving Australia, Rachel had been erratic and mean in ways that weren't like her and I was looking for explanations.

I found people online who said the medication had altered their loved one's personality. Some had seen partners go through startling changes to their core values. An anthropologist from New Jersey had written a dissertation on the exact medicine Rachel was taking, calling it *the falling-out-of-love drug*. She wrote that it affected some people after a couple of months of taking it. The whole thing seemed plausible. My progressive, feminist American fiancée had suddenly become a regressive money-driven seeker of patriarchal protection who wanted a rough lover. What else could explain it but chemicals?

During that time, I also made an appointment to see my sister's GP because I was forming a plan of action without really knowing it. I needed to act rather than think because none of the problems I had were the kind you could think your way out of.

★

Later that day, at the doctor's surgery, I explained what I was worried about. She was a GP I'd only seen once or twice before but she knew my sister, and I mentioned the Nembutal Theda had, while the GP slowly nodded.

'I understand why she would want that,' she said.

'I'm worried about the method,' I said. 'I listened to a radio show once about people who'd got this drug from a Mexican website. One of the women didn't die but gave herself brain damage. How do we know it's the right dose?'

The doctor rocked in her chair slightly, looked concerned and wrote something down.

A couple of hours later, I got a call I'd mostly been expecting. Euthanasia was illegal, and I had mentioned it to a medical professional who was sympathetic to my sister's desire to die but whose medical licensing board wouldn't be. I never would have implicated her if push came to shove, but I'd put her in a difficult position. Her profession demanded that she call the authorities, and she did. She called me first to apologise. 'I'm sorry,' she said. 'I truly understand why Theda wants to die, but I could lose my medical licence.'

'It's okay,' I said.

Later that day, Theda confronted me in the kitchen, leaning over the walker she'd used to get from her bedroom up the hallway. 'How could you?' she said, weeping. 'The police are threatening to come over. They might arrest Mum for letting it in the house.'

'It was an accident,' I said. 'I didn't go meaning to say anything.'

'You went to *my* doctor, for fuck's sake.'

I apologised and retreated to the outside couches. Rachel was right: I was too passive sometimes. At the same time, I was completely uncertain about what was the right thing to do, so I'd taken a soft approach.

Mum came out in the evening and told me she'd deflected the authorities. 'You can't tell anyone else,' she said.

I promised her I wouldn't.

★

The next day I had an appointment with my psychologist, a man named Eberhardt whom I'd started seeing a few months earlier at Rachel's behest. Rachel said I needed professional support dealing with some of the situations that came up in my family. Eberhardt knew my sister and mother because Theda had seen his partner, who was also a counsellor. Mum had seen Eberhardt a couple of years ago for a few months. He understood the situation was complicated.

I told him what I was thinking and that I needed advice. The cheapest accommodation in Albany, New York, was reasonable and I could go there, find out if I had any hope of saving the relationship with Rachel, and then find a town to write in for a while if it didn't work out. I had to see Rachel first – that was the point – but I'd recently enrolled in a university course in creative writing and it could keep me busy otherwise. I needed to get out of Perth too. I couldn't face the city and all it meant right now. Seeing Rachel in person scared me for some reason, but it would show the confidence that Rachel had said I needed. Perhaps some grand gesture was required at a time like this.

'What's a person supposed to do?' I said.

'What do you mean?'

'I just don't know how else to figure out what comes next.'

Eberhardt was German and a pragmatist. A week ago, he had asked if I wanted these sessions for free. I guessed he understood I'd just given up my job and was probably in crisis. I'd done this before – fled Perth and found my centre again by getting some space from things here. He also knew Theda wanted to die.

'I feel obligated to stop her,' I said, 'because I don't believe she's really tried all possible treatments yet.'

I think after that he understood staying was worse than going.

'Beware of Rachel,' he said. 'She's not predictable at the moment.'

Theda would have stopped me from going if she'd asked me to stay.

'Use that plane ticket, Minty,' she said. 'I'll call you if anything changes here. Don't worry.'

'I'll come back if you need me,' I said.

She looked relieved, and so did Mum. I think they sensed the problem I was causing by being there. I'd given Theda permission to die, but I was conflicted and unpredictable. I was going through my own calamity. I think they needed me to follow my own path for a while. Eberhardt had suggested I not tell Rachel I was coming. He said she'd only tell me not to. It felt strange to be so unsure about so many things and yet to choose an action in the middle of that uncertainty.

'You're not like other men,' Rachel had said to me in happier times. 'You talk about your feelings but you're not weak.'

It was true, and I felt it as I got on the plane to America. I felt like someone who'd made a gut decision in a situation where that was required. I felt courageous and scared, and like I'd done the right thing.

Two

Over the years, I've come to think of masculinity as a shadow. Growing up, I didn't have a word for it, but I understood it as a pressure that follows you around. It shames you if you step out of line. I remember arriving at high school with my best friend when I was thirteen. He was a freckle-faced kid called Benjamin Rand, whom I'd known since I was seven. Benjamin was in tune with that shadow. He loved Aussie Rules and war movies, and his father was a thick-necked, blue-eyed man in oil and gas. I saw the occasional cruel streak in Benjamin, but he was also sensitive and I connected with that, wondering if his boyishness was perhaps the thing I lacked.

I'd grown up playing hospitals and going birdwatching with fake binoculars, whereas Benjamin had grown up playing with pulleys and knives and army camouflage gear. I'd been dressed in wigs and high heels by a rambunctious older sister, whereas his older brother had shown him how to mix household chemicals to make miniature explosions. We were a good match in a way. He introduced me to things I didn't understand, and I offered a sensitivity that his real brother lacked.

My mother was doing her best at parenting. Looking back, I see her feminism in my childhood. I'm not sure she knew the term, because she'd never finished high school or gone to university, and her politics came from experience rather than books, but she was fierce about Theda being confident and me being soft. Mum had been taken out of school as a girl to work in a dress shop in England, whereas her brother got an education. Despite such sexism, she was a leader. She'd saved two people from drowning, provided cardiopulmonary resuscitation to car accident survivors and been used as a hostage in the women's prison where she'd worked after moving to Perth. She'd emigrated on a whim, with only seven pounds to her name, from a little country town in England to Western Australia, where she knew no one.

In our family, Dad had checked out by the time I was about ten. He lived in the same house, but we didn't see him much. He called Theda and me 'You Westerners' and told us we weren't Burmese enough. He was black and Mum was white, and Theda and I were more like Mum even though we looked half like Dad. So, rather than my father, it was Benjamin who introduced me to what was expected of a normal Aussie boy in the world's most isolated city.

I remember when Benjamin first got me listening to Metallica. It seemed absurd to call it music. I preferred classical. But my sense of the Shadow told me Benjamin knew something I needed to understand, and to be with him I had to pretend. He also needed me, which made me feel useful. He had a fragility I could see, even if he tried to deny it.

'Don't tell anyone,' he said when I found out about his bedwetting. 'It's a medical thing.'

'Of course,' I said. 'It's nothing to feel bad about.'

'Thank you. Thank you, Khin,' he said, and it made me feel buoyant. My desire to make Benjamin happier bonded us. I could see relief when I gave him gentler ways of looking at himself and the world. All it took was treating him like I had treated my sister growing up.

But when high school came, things changed. Benjamin quickly found a group he liked. I wasn't that concerned about sitting with his new friends in the first week. High school had many more kids than I was used to, and I was curious. I was walking down the corridor on my second day, feeling good, when a big kid shoved me. He then punched me in the face without a moment's thought. I was shocked. I'd never been hit like that before, yet I instinctively knew I couldn't tell anyone. That knowledge came from somewhere deep down in the machinery of an unconscious mind honed in a world that Benjamin understood better than me, but which I'd intuited from being around him.

Theda was a year ahead of me and went to a different high school, a selective school in the city that was more academic. I was starting to recognise that I needed *not* to show my smarts if I wanted to fit in as a boy. Boys who let their intelligence show became targets. Even in primary school I'd started to learn that, and I didn't have the nerve to push through. I wanted to fit in more than I wanted to impress the teachers. I'd been put into the gifted stream in primary school, but I'd dropped out because it was clearly un-Australian to the boys around me.

'Sorry, Khin,' Benjamin said, after a few weeks of high school. 'It isn't going to work. You should stop trying.'

'Can you say something?' I said. 'Maybe they'd let me join if you did?'

He shook his head before I could finish. 'You should sit with the Asians,' he said.

'The Asians?'

'On the oval. They all go out there and sit in the middle together. We can still hang out outside of school and all that.'

'But I'm not—'

'I know … I know,' he said, looking ashamed while also trying not to be overheard by anyone else in the corridor. 'I know you're not like those ones. I just think it would be better. Not just for me – better for *everyone*.'

It was a misunderstanding. It had to be, I figured. The Asian kids stuck together because they were alike, whereas I wasn't. They were graceful and quiet, but definitely *other*: they spoke with accents and answered questions in class whenever possible. They moved among us like silent fish in the hallways, weaving out of coral dominated by white kids, never making contact with anyone except each other. And they wouldn't have hesitated to tell a teacher if a kid had punched one of *them* in the face for no reason.

During lunchtime and recess, white kids took the two central quadrangles, surrounded by the school buildings, whereas the Asians collected their things from their lockers, went to the middle of a barely used oval a long way from everyone and out of sight. We didn't even see them again until classes began. They were like a different world we knew only from a distance.

As far as I understood it, they blended different grade levels when relaxing together. The kids I wanted to mix with were much more hierarchical than that. And while the Asian boys and girls might have sat together, that wasn't how the white kids did it. White kids sat gender-separated and were boisterous compared to the docile Asians who spoke in their whiny-nattery banter that the white kids called 'Chinese'. It was the language they spoke with their parents, I gathered. I didn't speak it.

I started to see the Asians as blameworthy because that was what everyone else did. Asian kids got notes from their parents to get out of Mr Taylor's physical education classes. I hated his sports class too, but hiding was against the Shadow that Benjamin had taught me. Sports were essential for showing that you were a man, and the Asians should have known better than to eat their strange, smelly foods and speak in a language other people didn't know while avoiding us. They seemed not to care about understanding the Shadow. I resented them for that because I didn't like it either but felt I had no choice. It's true that none had been born in Australia, and I didn't begrudge them that, but I thought they should have tried more. In my thirteen years of experience, I had figured out some of what was required to fit in, and it was hard. I didn't like the idea that some people could get away with ignoring it.

This racist attitude was reinforced by the white kids who had nothing but hatred for the Asians. Boys coughed the word *nip* into their hands as Asian students passed, and girls gossiped about how they smelled.

'It's a bit *nippy* in here, isn't it?' people said when the Asians walked into classrooms. The teachers were ignorant so long as they didn't get complaints. Maybe they turned a blind eye because it was easiest and the Asians, like my father, were masterful at just getting on with their lot. They were a 'model minority' not only because they were studious and self-sufficient but also because they didn't complain.

'All they care about is themselves,' people said. 'They want money. They're gunna take over this country without anyone even noticing.'

'They're like ants,' I overheard a popular girl say. 'Little robots. Mum says that's why they're so good at making circuit boards.'

'They're coons,' said Owen Brady, who hated everyone brown equally.

Mixing up racial epithets was typical back then. Slurs against non-whites were interchangeable because the complaint was essentially the same. And racist chatter was the basis of many conversations – it was the fallback if things wandered too far. Dislike of the Asians (and all they represented) was a sort of True North that could reorientate everyone. In a city where the local population recognised itself as minor – cut off from the rest of Australia by a desert larger than Western Europe – that hunger for a stone to grind against was even stronger than it might have been in other parts of the country.

'They don't care about real people,' Trent Clarke said. 'That's why they did all those things in the war. All of the wars. Vietnam. World War Two. Probably World War One as well.'

As the first year of high school rolled on, I couldn't get on board with all the Asian-bashing talk even if I resented the Asians for my own reasons. They had a community that I wasn't a part of, but they weren't threatening to me. When kids lumped me in with them, as Benjamin had, I assumed it was just an easy insult. Yes, I looked like an Asian, but how could people mistake me for one when I didn't have an accent or behave like one?

Another reason I wouldn't partake in slandering the Asians was because I loved my dad, despite how much he ignored me. Dad wanted Theda and me to be *more* Asian. He'd fought with Mum about it when we were young and still did sometimes when he bothered to talk to her. He said Burmese kids were better than Westerners, and he blamed any problems Theda and I had on our not being more Burmese. Even when we got sick with a cold, he would tell us it was because we weren't mindful enough, like Burmese Buddhist children.

Lastly, I wouldn't join in belittling the Asians because I didn't think my father had stolen anyone's job. That was the main complaint levelled at the Asians at school: that they were stealing white people's jobs. The phrase *They're gunna steal all the jobs!* was uttered more than any other phrase, among the boys in particular. My dad had come from Burma when he was twenty because a special aid program had brought him. That program had trained him to be a psychologist and now he worked with people in prisons. It was his job and he hadn't stolen it from anyone.

The White Australia policy had ended only a few years before most of us were born, but I didn't know this then. I didn't even know what the White Australia policy was. My parents never talked about racism, and I don't recall a single class at school that talked about Asian immigration, which is ridiculous because it was happening all around us. Stereotypes about Asians came from movies, TV and our imaginations because none of us ever talked to them, including me. Theda and I had only ever had white friends.

★

About a year after being denied entry to Benjamin's group of boys, a popular girl approached me in the corridors. She'd heard from someone that I thought she was attractive. Her fear was more obvious than what she said to me. She called me disgusting. She had gathered a large crowd to witness this. They had found me alone, as usual, sitting on a bench near the library.

'Don't even look at me,' she said. 'You're the most disgusting person in the whole school. Just looking at you makes me feel like puking my guts up.'

I wasn't upset about it. I knew I wasn't liked by then. During those first two years at high school, I laughed along or ignored it if kids called me racist names. If they broke my things, I avoided them in future. I pretended it was a mistake when they called me a nip or an Asian cunt. I found rubbish in my backpack but acted like it was a joke. Kids punched me but they also hit each other in play, so I pretended to myself it was friendly even when it wasn't in my case. If I saw my belongings in the urinal, I quickly retrieved them and washed them off. Once, someone told me that the eggs my parents had cleaned off their front windows last week were meant for me as a 'welcome to the neighbourhood' gift. I assumed they knew my address because of Benjamin.

But when that popular girl berated me, it nonetheless showed me something I wasn't comfortable facing. Her reaction to me was visceral, and she'd done something girls at our school didn't do – she'd amassed a crowd to come and witness her bullying a boy. Girls at Rossmoyne simply didn't behave that way towards any of the boys ever.

I felt it was my fault that I drew so much attention. After all, I was so clearly not like those Asian immigrants that if people said I was it indicated I'd slipped up. I'd messed up behaving right in some other way. Likening me to that hated group was due more to the convenience of ready-to-hand insults than anyone's actual belief that I was like them.

Theda was experiencing something similar at her school. I was aware of it, but she didn't discuss it with me. She was less present in my life than when we'd been little children. Her sexuality was blooming and she was obsessed with extracting pesky black Asian hairs from every part of her body. She'd asked me to call her Katie in the years leading up to high school. It hadn't stuck, so now she was concerned with other ways of fitting in with her peers. She was not pretty by 1980s Perth standards, which cast Asian girls as tainted. But looking back, I see that she was very pretty: slender, small-breasted and unique. There was something South Asian in her face. She had freckles when you looked closely. Her eyes were almond-shaped, her irises almost black.

She developed an eating disorder, and our parents started arguing about us again.

Dad told our mother she was ruining us by making us just like Westerners, whereas Mum argued that we were growing up in the West so that was okay. I just kept my head down and I think Theda did too, despite many of the arguments being about her.

During this time, Dad also started picking on me more. He mostly spent his time in the backyard in a little prefab room that he'd taken as his study, but at dinnertime he would come up to the house. As soon as he sat down, he'd begin to critique my way of eating. I didn't hold a knife and fork correctly or drink water mindfully enough. He'd lecture us about the Buddha and how Burmese values were based on religion. After he was gone, my mother would apologise for him. She'd tell me that boys were especially important in our father's culture and that's why he did it. But this made no sense, since he didn't show any other interest in me, and I didn't want to be like a Burmese boy anyway.

★

In 1989, Jack van Tongeren became a figure in Western Australia. We weren't the sort of family who watched the news, so I first heard of him from other kids while waiting on a slope of grass for Mr Taylor to return and assign football captains. Mr Taylor always took great pleasure in choosing two popular boys to be captains, and then he let them select their team members one by one. It meant I was always sitting alone at the end, and that said something to the others that encouraged their bullying. Mr Taylor laughed at the boys' bullying comments. There weren't any other Asian kids in Mr Taylor's class by then, so when people started talking about Van Tongeren, all eyes fell on me.

'Van Tongeren is just saying what people think,' a boy sitting near me said.

'Richardson's dad lost his fucking job to a nip,' replied Brad McCormick.

'I wanna know what Khin *Myint* thinks,' someone said.

I said I didn't know what they were talking about, and they told me that Jack van Tongeren had been burning down Chinese restaurants to make the nips go home. He'd been caught and sent to jail, but his friends were still doing something about the Asian problem.

'Your parents own a restaurant, right?' said Michael Young.

'My dad's a psychologist,' I said.

'Steal a job, did he?' said Richardson. 'That what your dad did?'

'Van Tongeren is a hero,' chimed in another before I could answer, and by now it was clear what the consensus was. 'He's saying what people are too afraid to say out loud but actually think!'

Following murmurs of agreement, I looked at Matt Richardson, who was glaring at me. Richardson was one of my worst bullies. He always sat next to me in science class and broke my pens. He encouraged the kids behind us to spit on me.

'I reckon that cunt Meredith is part of it,' Richardson said.

'Part of what?'

'That whole fucking group that want to free us of nips,' said McCormick. 'Another fucking hero right there.'

Just then, Mr Taylor returned.

As usual, I had nothing to do with the ball during the game. It came my way once by accident, and I was grateful when someone else picked it up. I watched the kid playing halfback and wondered why he was so different from me. He wasn't athletic, but the others gave him the ball and called out his name expectantly. Part of me wanted that too, even though I couldn't have cared less about football. I wanted them to call my name and look for me to pass the ball their way, even though they knew I wasn't a star athlete.

That night, I asked my mother about Van Tongeren. She said it was true that he had burned down Chinese restaurants. Nicholas Meredith – the other man they'd mentioned – had beaten a Malaysian taxi driver called Peter Tan to death one night. Meredith told the police he had done it because he hated Asians, and talked about that to the press at his trial.

'Those men are racists,' Mum said. 'It means they don't like Asian people.'

'People like us?'

'You're not Asian,' she said.

I would learn many years later that Van Tongeren was the leader of a group called the Australian Nationalist Movement. They'd plastered four hundred thousand posters around the Perth metro area with anti-Asian slogans like *Asians out or racial war!* and *Coloured immigration: a trickle now a flood*. They had a military-style training camp, fire-bombed several Asian restaurants and were heavily armed. I would also discover that Meredith was charged with manslaughter, not murder, and then given only three years in prison, despite having beaten Peter Tan and repeatedly jumped on his stomach for no reason other than racial hatred. Meredith's lawyers argued that Tan's head hit the curb during this unprovoked beating, which the judge accepted as a reason for giving the lesser sentence. Of course, part of being a model minority in Perth meant raising no protest about this.

I might not have properly understood the concept of racism as a child, but I started avoiding the sun. My skin was stubbornly chocolate, but sun made it darker like my father's cocoa complexion. Dad was approaching black in summer. He was the colour of Aboriginal men I'd seen on TV. I didn't want that, so I avoided the beach unless my mother insisted on a family trip, in which case I wore sunscreen and tried to sit in the shade the whole time.

I also began doing things that would show my manhood clearly. In class I acted out what I understood about the Shadow by talking back to the teachers. I once made the mistake of talking back to Mr Taylor, who quietly took me into his office, rolled up a sleeve and told me he'd punch me in the face if I ever did it again. I didn't understand Mr Taylor. He was the one teacher popular among boys who categorically disliked all teachers and yet he was the nastiest teacher of all.

I was also angry with my parents during this time for a reason that I knew wasn't fair. Mixed-race children weren't illegal, but why had my parents thought it was a good idea to bring my sister and me into existence? There was a reason I never met any half-Asian kids or even Asians born in Australia. My parents should have known better than to do something like that. I didn't understand why they seemed unaware of what a drastic mistake it had been. When I was a boy, Mum had wanted to enter Theda and me into a modelling competition. When I remembered this, I couldn't believe how naive my mother was for thinking Theda and I would ever be considered anything but dirty in some way.

I pleaded with my mother to stop cooking Eastern foods, lest I smell.

'But you love curries,' Mum said.

'My tastes have changed,' I protested. 'I want normal food. What about what Benjamin's mum used to cook?'

Mum looked at me sceptically. She'd gone to night school to learn Asian recipes so her exotic husband might feel at home in a Western country, and now I was rebelling against a cuisine I'd always said was to my liking. She could see it was a lie, yet she didn't understand why it mattered.

Despite my frustration, I never fell out with Mum. Perhaps it was because I sensed her unhappiness in Australia too. She didn't like the local culture and told me she felt trapped in this country. I often found her crying in her room in the evenings, and she'd say she missed England, where people were supposedly less 'harsh' than in Western Australia.

I remember Dad kicked a hole in Theda's bedroom door around this time. It was just before he became even more withdrawn, retreating to his demountable in the backyard as soon as he arrived home from work and staying there until well after midnight each weekday. On weekends we didn't see him at all. He practised Buddhism and ignored us as much as possible, but Theda's eating disorder was an issue that needed dealing with. My parents installed locks on the kitchen doors, and in outrage I learned to pick them.

I started going into the kitchen after everyone else had gone to bed. I'd retrieve a little paring knife with a wooden handle from the kitchen drawer and take it back to my bedroom, where I would drag its tip over the soft flesh of my inner wrist. I didn't want to die. Imagining what it might feel like to get out of existence altogether was a fantasy I indulged in for its own sake, and the knife was just a prop.

'I don't like Australia,' Theda confided to me after a particularly nasty argument between our parents. 'We aren't Australian. We're like Mum. I want to go back to England.'

'We were never in England,' I said.

She looked troubled and said something about Mum possibly being wrong for teaching us not to speak with Australian accents.

It was a troubled time for our family. When I went to comfort Mum if I heard her crying, she'd talk about money. I didn't realise until later that she was thinking about leaving Dad but faced a situation many mothers did. She wasn't university-educated and hadn't worked full time since having children.

'Khin,' she said many times, 'don't ever get into this position. Make sure that you're financially independent.'

Sometimes she'd tell me that she felt like killing herself. Part of me worried she would.

Not long after that, my parents divorced but didn't move into different houses. Mum didn't have the money for it. Instead, they built a fence down the middle of the garden and nailed shut one internal door, dividing our medium four-bedroom house into two. We lived on both sides. It was an odd arrangement. Theda and I would go over to Dad's half of the house for dinner, and it was like visiting little Burma over there. Dad had a large iron Buddha statue in the corner and wooden trinkets depicting various objects that I'd never seen in Australia. We would eat dinner on a sheet on his floor, wash up in the adjoining bathroom's shower recess and then return to Mum's side of the house, where she had decorative English plates on the walls.

'When Dad first came to Australia,' Theda told me once as we walked around to Dad's side, 'he didn't know how to use a knife and fork.'

'What do you mean?' I asked.

'Burmese people eat with their hands. He spilled peas on the floor and then rubbed them into the carpet with his feet, hoping no one would notice.'

I understood my father a little better after that. Part of me realised he was ashamed of his Burmese upbringing. He constantly criticised the whiteness in Theda and me but was also jealous of it. Theda told me other things, such as that my parents had struggled to get an apartment when they married because Perth landlords didn't like that Dad was Asian.

'Mum would go looking for something because Dad was at work,' Theda said. 'They'd tell Mum she could have the apartment and to come back with her husband to sign the papers, but then they'd see Dad and say it was already taken.'

I think Theda felt sorry for our father, as well as resenting him for abandoning and constantly criticising us. By then, he had become a Buddhist zealot and used Buddhist teachings to show us we were inferior to the Burmese values he had fought for us to have.

'I fucking hate mindfulness,' Theda said to me more than once.

Mum was even more hostile towards Buddhism. After the separation from Dad, she would curse the Buddha. I think it was easiest for her to blame the religion for her ex-husband's behaviour. 'The Buddha was a selfish bastard,' she used to say. 'Left his wife and children in pursuit of his own selfish enlightenment, just like your father.'

Whenever she said this, I would look anxiously at the chipboard nailed over what had once been the door connecting the living room to the master bedroom. The chances that my father was over in his bedroom were slim because he was almost always in the prefab, but I feared he would hear it if he was. I wasn't afraid he'd be angry at Mum. I was scared of something else. I think I was worried about his fragility.

That chipboard was thin, and you could hear everything from the other side. The fence dividing our garden was more substantial. It was made of gapless red planks of thick wood, and it was higher than any of the fences separating the properties on our street. If Dad was in his little prefab on the other side of that fence, sitting barefoot in one of his longyis, as he often was, he wouldn't hear a thing.

Three

Outside Terminal 4, a recorded voice welcomed us to JFK International Airport with the exuberance of late-night talk show host introducing a celebrity guest. It was my first hint that I'd entered a culture full of the clichés that I knew from movies but which are so strange to encounter in real life. I'd left Perth thirty-six hours earlier and should have been exhausted, but I was wide awake.

Passengers were flowing around me, heading for cabs under a large awning, as I stood near the exit. It seemed remarkable that you could step out of one climate directly into another. I'd left a place where the air was dry and cool for a city thick with humidity. I could have stood in shorts and a t-shirt if I'd wanted to, despite it being after midnight.

I saw some smokers huddled near one of the pillars and went to stand near them so I wouldn't get in anyone's way. I had quit cigarettes again, thank god, since deciding to come here. Smoking rarely troubled me these days, but stress sometimes made me reach for a nicotine crutch as it had after Rachel's sudden departure. As I watched people calling out to their rides, I thought about how Rachel had told me that foreigners' criticisms of Americans were misguided. 'You have to be assertive in my country,' she'd said. 'Yes – Americans are loud, but that's because the US is like a massive dinner table, and if you don't bang your spoon you won't get fed.'

I looked over at a line of people being shuffled into waiting cabs. I'd planned virtually nothing beyond my arrival. I had a place to stay for three days in Manhattan, then a month booked at a cheap B & B up in Albany. I'd told Eberhardt and Mum that I might stay on in America for the duration of my visa, even if Rachel rejected me, but I hadn't been sure I would do it until that moment. Looking at the buzz around me, I was certain that I would stay. It felt like being in a different world, and that was comforting. A lot of the people I saw were black or brown, which also gave me a good feeling.

'You live in one of the whitest places I've ever seen,' Rachel had told me upon moving to Perth. It was the first thing she'd noticed. 'Maybe it's just Fremantle, but Fremantle is the progressive hub of your city, right?'

Racial identity politics wasn't something I'd let my mind entertain before meeting her. The few times I'd spoken to friends in Perth about race and my childhood, I'd been shut down.

I'd moved back to Perth in my mid-twenties after a four-year stint in Melbourne, and I didn't have old high school friends so had effectively started over. I was an adult trying to make friends in a city I'd grown up in. Part of my strategy had been moving to Fremantle. No one was overtly racist there, but it was very white and people constantly asked where I was from. I usually said only that my mother was British. I was still ashamed of my Asian roots. But the progressives of Fremantle weren't happy with that answer. 'No, but, like, I mean ...' they would flounder, unsure how to reframe the question. 'You've, like, got something else, right?' I would then explain that my father was from Burma, hoping they'd not linger on the fact. It took me a while to recognise that they found it exotic rather than disgusting. But if I ever tried to talk to people in my new neighbourhood about racism, they suddenly switched gears. They said things like 'Asians do pretty well for themselves, don't they? ... I think of you as white now that I know you anyway ... Do you really think Perth is racist?'

I was glad that people in Fremantle supposedly thought of me as white once they knew me, but it could be stifling. Many times I nodded along as groups of locals bonded over supposedly universal Australian childhood experiences. I wouldn't talk about my own experiences because it would have broken the illusion. It also would have meant talking about racism, which put some people on the back foot, no matter how progressive they imagined they were. Their response implied that I was trying to be difficult, or that I thought I was special somehow and needed to be put in my place – 'Everyone has troubles … we don't all go around blaming racism.'

When Rachel criticised Fremantle, she talked about its colourblind attitude as hypocritical. She had learned critical race theory in university. She'd done a degree that sounded different from what I'd encountered at university back in the '90s, when postmodernism was so fashionable and pretentious that it obscured all meaning.

'What exactly *is* an identity?' I'd asked her once.

'It's how people perceive you. It's also how you perceive yourself. It's both. Women are socialised to be people pleasers, so that's how they act. It's the same with race. If you're black, the culture perceives you a particular way, and it affects how you feel about yourself.'

Ideas like that were so intuitively true when I heard them, and yet Australian culture was concerned with pretending things like class and race didn't exist, so I hadn't allowed myself to dwell on those ideas when they occurred to me independently. Asian claims of victimhood were particularly suspect. White people thought all Asians were Chinese or Malaysian and became lawyers or doctors.

When I told Rachel that hearing her talk about race like that hit home with me, she was surprised at first. She'd not thought much about the Asian experience. But as I explained it, she began to sell America to me as a place where I would fit in.

'You don't belong in Australia,' she said after a few months in my hometown. 'You'll fit in better in my country. You'll be able to talk how you want about your experiences.'

Rachel said that Americans imagined Australian culture as laid-back when it really wasn't. This was something she'd felt after living in my country for a while. She said Australians had a way of talking that hid their uptightness. 'It's all – *No worries. All good, mate. No drama.* That's how Australians do it. Whenever I start talking about anything uncomfortable, they scatter dismissive slang like that, as if they're tossing grenades, desperately trying to stop me.' At this point, she would usually pause and tell me that I was different from other Australians.

Rachel's impressions of Perth had tainted her impression of Australia as a whole, but I didn't bother to defend it. I'd felt alienated from it for as long as I could remember. The idea that her country might feel more like home was appealing.

★

In the cab to Manhattan, I looked out at a flood of traffic as we moved through some unrecognisable part of the city. I'd seen this place in movies and TV shows my whole life, but none of that was real. Nestled into the crooks of exit ramps were tower blocks where I glimpsed actual lives, hung off balconies in the form of damp towels and clothing. Greater New York City's unspecified masses were churning.

'People have all sorts of opinions about my country when they haven't even been there,' Rachel had told me. 'America is much more than its movies.'

I tried to imagine how many different lives existed in those buildings. I would see this country through Rachel's eyes now. Maybe I would understand her better because of that. She had so easily shifted her mindset once she'd arrived back here. Perhaps the place allowed such a thing. Maybe the version of her I'd known in Australia had been artificial because it wasn't here, where she'd grown up?

As we reached Manhattan, rain started to fall. My driver slowed down and I watched the people on the sidewalks. They hailed cabs with long, straight arms. The expressions on their faces embodied firm intent acquired in a city where you have to push your way through things. Women laughed with their heads back and high as rain sizzled on concrete and pedestrians dove for cover under awnings. A homeless man with a cardboard sign sat getting drenched as a translucent braid of water roped down the shopfront window beside him.

'One hundred six, and four?' my driver asked through a tinny intercom speaker.

'That's right,' I said.

What happened next was a shot across the bow. The excitement I'd felt a moment earlier vanished and was replaced with gut-wrenching anxiety as I checked all my pockets and backpack for my wallet, which wasn't there. My mind began to race. I calculated the time in Perth. The only recourse I had would be calling Mum and asking her to wire some money. Even if I figured out how to make a reverse-charge call, she rarely picked up the phone. And who knew if she'd even be able to help?

I scanned the scene outside, wondering if a person could sleep in the subway.

★

Ten minutes later, I was on the sidewalk of a quiet street in the Upper West Side with forty crumpled dollars in my hand. My wallet was gone, but my cash had been in my money belt. A travel agent back in Perth had suggested I store some local money in a place other than my wallet. She had also sold me a currency card onto which I could transfer some money.

At 1.30 a.m., in a cramped little lobby that smelled of paint, I transferred two thousand dollars from my bank account onto the currency card. It would take three days to clear, but I had the forty dollars, so I'd be okay for food if I was careful.

Before going up to my room, I paused in front of a TV bolted onto the archway above an elevator. On screen, a dapper man and a slick, attractive woman were orchestrating an extended analysis of a trial. I had spent the last hour cancelling cards and sending emails to airlines – but this one story had been going the whole time. Now I was paying more attention and wondering what was so important that it got this much attention. The news anchors kept mentioning Trayvon Martin. I wasn't sure if he was the victim or the perpetrator, but someone was dead.

A scene from the day's trial began to play. A white lawyer in his sixties was addressing a black woman in a witness box. She was youngish, in her twenties maybe, and heavy, with oversized gold hoops dangling from her ears.

'What makes that racial?' he said.

'What makes that *racial?*' she repeated back, screwing up her face as if she thought he might be a moron.

'What makes that racial?' he asked again, unfazed.

The scene flipped back to the news studio, where the breathless anchors were hosting several talking heads on video feeds.

'What you have to understand, Terry,' one talking head said to another, 'is that growing up black in the inner-city means you live in a com-*pah*-leetly different America.'

'Come on now, Rebecca,' Terry replied condescendingly, 'we all live in the *same* America.'

I listened for a while with a growing feeling that I was witnessing what Rachel had said my country lacked. It was poetic: somehow on my first night in America, I had stumbled across one of the things Rachel had informed me would give me a good feeling about this country, something that spoke deeply to me.

I wished Theda could have seen it. The talking heads were arguing about whether racial identity affects how people understand themselves. It was a debate, and both sides thought they were right. But how validating it was just to hear it happening! I was sure my sister would have felt the same. The idea that a nation would debate the existence of racial inferiority complexes on a mainstream news channel for an extended period of time meant something to me. Rachel had predicted it, but I hadn't understood the impact it would have on me until now. Rachel was right; it created a feeling of belonging.

At 2.30 a.m., I pulled myself away from the endless news and found my room. It was a dirty and smelly dormitory. A man sleeping on the bunk below mine was wearing his sneakers and snoring. I fell asleep listening to him and to the sounds of the street outside, feeling happy for the first time since Rachel had left me.

Four

The tension coursing through Rossmoyne peaked when I was in the middle of Year 10. A culture of fistfights was taking hold among the white boys, and I knew someone would challenge me soon. The fights were complicated things. They were proof of manliness, but they didn't follow the logic of courage. It would always be a tougher boy challenging a weaker one. A challenger presented a real dilemma for his victim. It would be a public beating if you accepted, and I'd attended a couple of after-school fights and had seen what happened. Everyone circled you, blocking every exit so you had to face fists and knees and kicks. But turning down the aggressor wasn't an easy or simple decision. It undermined your dignity so badly with the Shadow that bullying would likely get worse.

Later in life, I would read Judith Butler, who wrote that gender is our most fundamental category of identity and that deviance from it is so scary because it undermines our membership in the category 'human'. Not to be considered human is about as dangerous as things get for anyone. In frontier cultures, gender norms are homogenous and rigid and require constant maintenance. You can travel a hundred kilometres from Perth and find yourself in the middle of nowhere. To be part of a city like ours, you had to prove yourself as honourable and tough – at least that's what was sold to us boys. Not being tough and brave was tantamount to being subhuman and disposable.

That, more than anything else, was why I decided to try sitting with the Asians one lunchtime after two years of avoiding them – I wanted to be free of the expectation to be a fighter in a fight that I knew would reach me soon.

I approached the large group in the middle of the oval at lunchtime, fifty or more kids forming a moving matte of thick black hair against the green grass. A smiling girl, someone I'd spoken to once or twice in class, beckoned me over. After checking that she had my name right, the first question she asked was where in Asia I was from.

It took me aback. I didn't like that my Asian features were so obvious to her.

I asked what language they all spoke.

'We speak different languages,' the girl said laughing. 'The Australians think we all come from China, but we are from many places. Yes – we all are migrants. But Asia is very big. What about you?'

'I'm not Asian,' I said, then realised that wasn't something I needed to say here and backtracked. 'I'm half,' I said. 'My father is from Burma and my mum is English.'

The girl asked if my father was a refugee, and I didn't know how to respond.

'Can he return to Burma?' she asked gently.

I told her no, and she nodded like she understood.

I knew the story from my mother mostly. Dad had been let into Australia for the aid program on the proviso that he go back when it was over. It was a golden opportunity. He was from a poor village, and the idea of getting a university education in the West must have seemed like a dream come true. But when he met my mother and they married, the Australian government tried to boot him out. The Burmese government had taken his passport and threatened his family in Burma. The whole thing had been very knife's edge in terms of the life we'd ended up with.

'How do you know about Burma?' I said, when the conversation drifted away from my family. Several of the other Asian kids were talking about how Burma was a dangerous country and its people oppressed. I had rarely met teachers who knew where Burma was, so hearing people my own age discuss its political situation was unusual.

'Of course we know about Burma,' one of them said. 'It's in Asia, and we are all Asian!'

As they talked more, I learned that they were mostly from Malaysia, Singapore and China. They hadn't met a mixed-race person before me. Nor had they met anyone from Burma, or an Asian person born in Australia. Most had come over as little children.

Asian students were less attention-grabbing than the white boys in the quadrangles, who were performative and constantly trying to show each other up. They masked it as humour, each one taking a turn in the limelight and making fun of someone before handing over to the next. I knew this about the white boys because I so often watched them from the outside, since I was mainly a loner in their spaces.

The Asians, on the other hand, seemed less about the individual and more about balanced collective conversation. Everyone was involved and no one was ridiculed. I realised that I was being accepted without question and had spent years judging these kids unfairly.

Earlier that week, I'd seen an Asian boy pretending he didn't understand English as white boys ridiculed him in the corridor. He was sitting near me now, speaking perfectly competent English. The Asian kids' way of dealing with hatred from the white kids was to make themselves distant. They stuck together because it wouldn't have made sense not to stick together.

'It must make it easier,' the girl who'd invited me over said gently.

'Easier how?'

'With the Australians,' she said. 'Being only half. We are *full* Asian, so they do not accept us.'

Just before lunch ended, someone made a joke and the little patch of kids I'd been sitting with reverted to whatever Asian language they had in common. The girl admonished them, saying, 'We should keep the conversation in English, for Khin. It's not polite to speak in our home language, because he only speaks English.'

★

The next day, I returned to the corridors with a strange mix of emotions. I felt good about myself for once. And yet it was more apparent to me than ever that I didn't belong with the Asians. They'd been kind, but I was an imposition on them. They hadn't said so, but they wanted to speak in their own languages. At least, I felt they would once the novelty of me wore off. They would be too polite to say anything, and I'd feel awkward. They were also extremely studious and talked about home and family in ways I couldn't relate to.

I was determined to take responsibility for my social failures with the white boys. I had watched them for years and they didn't doubt themselves like I did. At lunchtime, I headed towards where I knew Benjamin and his friends were. He was a kind of ally if I could get some traction with the people around him. A group like his offered safety. One of the popular boys had recently challenged someone in Benjamin's group to an after-school fight, and instead of subjecting him to the usual collective ridicule, people had hung back in their judgements. Benjamin's friend had then unexpectedly won the fight. I'd observed the effect. Benjamin's friend was invited to sit with the popular boys afterwards. He'd gracefully joined them for a week before returning to Benjamin's little cadre.

I found them in a little locker alcove near the boys' toilets. A flaxen-haired kid named Peter Catalina was on his feet when I approached. The other four boys were sitting on a bench against the wall, listening to him.

As soon as Catalina saw me, his face broadened into a grin. 'I smell Asian,' he said, sniffing the air in my direction.

'What's up?' I said, ignoring him.

Catalina giggled. 'Tell me, *Aung*. Did you eat curry last night like you do every night?'

Benjamin was watching us. These boys knew I had a Burmese name that I didn't use, and for a few months each year I would get shit about it. Maybe Benjamin had told them about it, or maybe they had heard it from a teacher. Teachers who didn't know me often used it because it was on my paperwork. I hated the sound of it – *Aung* – it sounded like a smell, and I resented my parents for not realising that giving me a name like that was a bad move.

'I don't eat curry,' I said.

Two other boys on the bench sniggered. 'It's true,' said Benjamin. 'His mum is from England.'

Catalina looked at me and licked his lower lip. 'Where's your kind from then?' he said.

'My kind?'

'As in which country in nip-land are you from?'

'My dad is from Burma,' I said. 'But my Mum is English. And I was born here.'

'No you fucking weren't,' Catalina said. 'So what? Are you some kind of half-breed?' I heard more sniggers from the bench and Catalina added, 'How did your Asian dad get a white woman to fuck him?'

I looked at him then for the first time. Until that moment, I'd been trying to look past him as if he weren't there. The group was what I cared about, not Catalina. I hadn't known him or even spoken to him before this. He was just doing what everyone seemed to do with me – hating who I was for a reason I didn't understand.

Until that day, no one had ever heard me speak back to a bully. My mother, in her glorious naivete, had drilled into me that ignoring bullies was the best answer you could give them. Being a gentle kid, I had followed that advice for much longer than some kids might have. Now something in me was silently getting ready to answer Catalina.

I turned to the boys on the bench. Benjamin looked uncomfortable.

One of the boys on the bench asked Catalina what he was doing, and I turned back to see for myself. He had begun miming something. It was like he was lifting an invisible bucket from between his legs, knees bent, with a constipated look on his face, and he was grunting. 'I'm doing the Vietnamese mating dance,' he said. 'The one that Khin's dad used to get a white woman to fuck him.'

What followed came from somewhere unexpected inside of me. It was a rational choice rather than an emotional response. At least that's how it felt, because for the first time in my life I pondered whether violence was a necessary part of the Shadow.

I knew it wasn't my desire to be violent, in part because I feared retaliation and didn't think of myself as someone capable of dealing with that. I could barely kick a football, let alone win a fight. But I knew sometime soon I would be challenged. Like many boys, I would face a decision about what to do, and that had preoccupied me for the past few months. Earlier that year, I'd seen a boy kicked in the stomach, doubled over, kneed in the face repeatedly and punched to the ground. Fights had a scent to them. They were bloody but it was more than that. They smelled like a kind of fear that was worse than the fight itself. The fights were getting to be regular; there were usually one or two a week.

I can pinpoint the exact moment I decided, with all of this in the back of my mind, to strike Catalina. What I discovered that day was that violence is like a switch. You can flick it over with the lightest touch of your finger if you dare, without even raising a sweat, and once it gets going, the electricity it produces is much more intense than the energy used to turn it on.

Childhood bullying and violence are rarely directly life-threatening. It's ostracism that makes a victim feel desperate. If most of your peers want you to suffer on an ongoing basis, the effect is a growing feeling of shame, and it becomes intolerable. It's the shame that's potentially life-threatening.

I was already scraping a knife over my inner wrist some nights. Mum was crying most evenings. She talked about wishing she was dead sometimes. Dad seemed to hate Theda and me for being too Western, and the kids at school despised me for being too Eastern. I felt like I had run out of options.

I also felt a sort of righteous anger for the Asians. They had been the only kids who'd been nice to me in years, and here was Catalina berating them, my father and me all at once.

I flipped a switch that day because I thought it would distance me from the Asian inside myself. If I wanted to be a white boy, I would need to prove it like this. I was tired of feeling unsafe. And although I knew my mother would never have approved, nor did she understand anything about what it was to be a boy growing up. So not out of anger but out of the need to be accepted, I beat Catalina until he was a mess on the floor.

★

I was suspended. A few days after I returned to school, a boy approached me in the woodwork corridor and, instead of offering friendship, had brought a large audience with him. He wanted to fight and I felt I had no choice. I also felt that I needed to prove myself one more time.

I won that fight.

After two more fights, I realised it wouldn't stop. I was different to the boy who'd been offered a way into the popular group after fending off a bully. Also, Catalina had told the teachers about my attack on him, which was against the rules of the Shadow as I knew them. But it was me being punished.

In the next two weeks, I was attacked twice more. I lost both fights because I refused to fight back.

After that, people went back to breaking my things, spitting on me and calling me names. I'd undone everything and was back on the bottom rung. Only now I was more conspicuous.

Five

The forty dollars I had was enough to eat from the food carts in New York City until the funds cleared from my bank account onto my currency card. I bought a decent meal and a bus ticket to Albany just as my hostel accommodation ran out.

The ride upstate was pretty. I looked out of a bus window at crumbling concrete structures that gave way to rusty silos, swathes of greenery and picturesque farms. I'd never imagined a tropical-like climate in the northern parts of North America. For everything Rachel had told me about her home state, she'd never mentioned that it got humid, only that it snowed in the winter.

When we reached Albany, I saw it was smaller than I'd expected. Rachel had talked about it synonymously with the Capital District, and I had been expecting a bustling city, but Albany was fairly minor. It had skyscrapers and a downtown grid, but it wasn't even as big as Perth.

My cab driver quizzed me about surfing and *Crocodile Dundee* as we drove past large parks with statues of soldiers on horseback, brandishing swords, next to people in suits or dresses eating lunch beside their briefcases on clipped grass. It reminded me that I was in the state capital. I wasn't sure about the location of my accommodation because I'd booked everything quickly before leaving Australia, with cost as the main factor. When we drove out into the suburbs, I was surprised. We pulled up outside a big old colonial mansion opposite a police precinct on one corner and a library on another.

I used an entry code to get in and found my room on the top floor in an attic space large enough for a family. Downstairs the old house was remarkably maintained. It was wooden with high ceilings and a sweeping staircase. I was alone – the manager had said she wasn't expecting other guests and wouldn't be around herself until the following day or the day after that. Arriving at a B & B without anyone present was slightly eerie, and it demonstrated such faith on the part of the management. I liked the sensation. I felt trustworthy and autonomous.

Since arriving in America, I'd felt that there was more space around me. In New York, I hadn't even had a room to myself but because of my distance from the troubles back home it had felt like stepping into a field, even on the busy streets. Being at Mum's house was like being buried under soil. Now I could smell the attic's wood, and the attic space was large, with a desk by a window, a little couch and a bed, and it was heaven.

★

After settling in, I went out to find a supermarket. I stood at the shelves smelling some scented candles for what must have been about ten minutes. When I wasn't in Perth, my personality shifted. I'd noticed it before. I became more feminine. It was as though part of me that couldn't afford to be out in Perth emerged when I was away.

Before returning to my room, I slipped into the pharmacy, got some antihistamines and saw cigarettes on sale. The jarring reality of addictive poison on sale alongside medicines reminded me of Rachel's characterisation of her country's capitalism. She'd said that for all the things she loved about it, US culture was ruthless and favoured independence over common sense a lot of the time.

On my way back to my room, I crossed the car park and overheard two women excited to see each other.

'Livi!' one of them screeched. 'I don't friggin bee-*lieve* it! You're, like, the perfect-fucking-person right now!'

It made me think of Rachel again. She had their same intonation. That was her I'm-so-happy-to-see-you singsong, and I had loved it. It made me feel special on a daily basis.

'Why wouldn't I let someone know when I'm excited to see them?' Rachel had admonished me when I'd mentioned it.

The funny thing was that I almost matched it in the end. It wasn't hard to dial up some extra excitement, especially if the goal was to make someone you liked feel good. I even tried it on my Australian friends and noticed them responding positively. I was learning new tricks from my foreign partner – tricks I imagined came from her culture.

But since losing her, I'd been pondering US culture more critically. I still couldn't make sense of that baffling final conversation. Rachel had seemed excited while breaking up with me: They were at the top of their field, Khin, from *New York City!*

During her visit to Perth, Mary had spoken to Rachel with the same ramped up enthusiasm on certain topics, especially on the subject of Rachel's future career. It was nice, encouraging like a crowd warm-up guy. After listening to Mary do it for a few days, I began to imagine the only thing keeping Rachel from the US presidency was time. But what else came bound up with such positivity?

Mary had opened up about something during that visit, something whispered to Rachel when I wasn't around. Rachel's dad was suffering from a chronic anxiety disorder. He had done for his whole life, and Rachel hadn't known. He was slated for electroshock therapy this year to try to improve it.

'It makes sense,' Rachel told me quietly in our bedroom after learning the truth. 'He used to hide away when my brother and I were little. He would stay in his room for days and we had to be very quiet around the house. Mom said he had migraines. But he was having panic attacks. I can't understand why she kept it from us.'

I remember looking for a way to soothe her sense of betrayal. 'Maybe she thought she was protecting you?' I said.

She looked at me with a troubled expression. 'It's the same problem I had,' she replied. 'I was on medication for anxiety in high school. Knowing about Dad might have helped.'

We had talked a little bit about the possibility that it was genetic, and she had nodded to herself slowly before saying, 'It flares up when his boss is pressuring him. I wish he could just quit.'

Rachel's dad was a high achiever, like Rachel. He was a brain–computer interface software engineer, which sounded like science fiction to me, though Rachel assured me it was world-changing and very real.

As I walked back to my accommodation in Albany, I wondered if American culture's outward positivity often hid deep pressure. High expectations had hurt Rachel's father, but Mary was trying the same script on Rachel: be amazing because you are amazing, honey – come back to America and change the world.

I couldn't stop myself from speculating a bit. I wondered if the American Dream had played a part in my relationship ending like it did.

★

Back at the B & B, I cooked and then went up to my room. And after dark, I sent Rachel an email. It was three short paragraphs that I'd shown to Eberhardt and my mother before leaving and both had said it was good. I hoped so. I told her that I didn't expect her to meet me but figured she might since I had come so far. I explained I'd already bought the plane ticket by the time she'd told me not to come, even though she already knew that. I explained that I needed closure.

After dark, the little flip phone I'd bought down in New York City jangled to life and I thought Rachel was already calling, but it was Mum.

'The internet says Albany is twelve hours ahead,' she said.

'Behind,' I said.

'Do you have a nice room?'

'Yeah. So nice.'

After that, she told me about a neurologist Theda was booked in to see. It was in four weeks' time. It was the same story as always – they hoped this doctor would help where others had failed. Theda had migraines at the moment. When she had them, she often couldn't sleep and I worried about the possibility of a psychosis.

'Keep an eye out for it,' I said.

Mum registered the point but changed the subject.

'Do you have Olanzapine?' I asked, ignoring her deflection.

'I don't think so.'

I felt a wave of frustration.

'I'll get some,' she said, then quickly changed topic again.

'Will you get some tomorrow?' I asked.

'She won't take them if she's psychotic,' Mum said, as if that were an excuse not to try.

'I thought you said she wasn't psychotic yet?'

'I just … okay. I'll get some.'

'If she gets psychotic and refuses, crush them up and put them in some food,' I said.

Mum stammered a bit, then agreed.

I felt chastened after the call. Rachel's family had a don't-tell policy about mental illness but my own family's attitude to Theda's psychotic breaks was flat-out denial sometimes. If Theda got psychotic while I was away, I would have to return. She'd attacked our mother last time. The psychotic breaks were nothing we could afford to downplay.

The phone rang again, and this time it was Rachel. Her voice was childish. 'Are you really here?'

I said I was.

'Let's meet,' she said. 'Tomorrow.'

She described a cafe just out of town and then unexpectedly laughed when I asked if I would find it on Google Maps. It was a running joke that I was tech dumb.

Six

Fights on school grounds were scary, but after-school fights were worse. After-school fights meant big crowds, and the violence often got out of hand. I was much more afraid of them because of that, and I was finally challenged to one by Brad McCormick and Liam Murphy a few weeks after the incident with Catalina had blown over. A messenger gleefully explained during recess that it wasn't something I could avoid because the whole student population would help Brad and Liam track me down. They were our grade's top dogs and most-liked boys. The pretty white girls dated them and all the boys wanted to be them. It made no sense that they were targeting someone as abject as me, jointly at that, but the messenger just shrugged and said that no one cared if it was unfair because it was payback for Catalina.

'Everyone – *everyone* – will be keeping an eye on you,' he said. 'It doesn't matter if you walk home a different way. People will be watching for you and letting them know. McCormick said that they aren't gunna give up until they get you. I'd just face it.'

I would understand much later that my situation was political in nature. bell hooks wrote that poor and working-class boys tend to use violence as the currency of status because it's the cheapest and easiest way of asserting manhood. White kids at Rossmoyne High used it that way. Violence and status were inextricably bound up with each other.

I heard Perth sold the highest number of Harley Davidsons per capita globally that year. And I represented something that kind of manhood couldn't accept: an Asian boy who thought he belonged with the whites and was willing to perform white masculinity to get that. It didn't matter that I'd since abandoned the whole idea; the fact was I'd once beaten a well-liked white boy for denigrating my half-caste racial status and I needed to be pushed back down. I'd had the audacity to transgress the divide the white boys were deeply invested in. They hated 'the Asians', but that category was also integral to how they defined themselves. I represented the dissolving boundary those kids and their families wanted to keep in place, with them at the top.

In the coming decades, Asians would become the majority at Rossmoyne High. In their way, those bogan kids had been right about the change that was coming. But I never once met another half-Asian in the small world I lived in. I never once saw mixed-race families. I never once met another Asian person whose only spoken language was English. Theda and I were the only ones, and we were monsters for it. We unsettled the world around us in some fundamental way that we couldn't understand or come to terms with. Theda and I had no way of understanding our situation as political, so we experienced it as shame instead. We lacked the language and concepts to make sense of it, and so did our parents.

'Will you go?' a boy in my math class asked after recess. The teacher had stepped out and a little crowd was surrounding me.

'Just tell them I don't want to fight,' I said. The boys and girls gathering around me confirmed this wasn't an option.

At lunchtime, I moved between the school's least used areas hoping to avoid detection.

When Liam saw me, he had about fifty others with him. Rather than speeding up, he slowed down. He altered his gait to mimic Rocky Balboa in the scene where he's about to enter the ring, and it brought forth a couple of whoops. I fled for the library. Terrified.

For the next half hour, little convoys of boys came in to tell me that Liam was waiting outside. I could see him on the bench. They also urged me to go outside so I might hear his challenge, which they reminded me was non-negotiable – the fight was inevitable.

After the lunch bell, I waited until the corridor was clear and went to my next class, which was computing, and sat next to a boy called Glen. Glen was popular enough but was one of the few white kids who had only ever been nice to me. It was serendipitous because I wouldn't have asked anyone else what I asked him. First I asked if he knew about the fight and he nodded.

'Whaddaya gunna do?' he said.

'Maybe I could ask Catalina to say something?'

'It's not about Catalina,' he said. 'That's what they're saying, but it's not.'

I remember taking stock before asking my next question. I realised afterwards that the question itself scared me.

'I don't understand', I said haltingly, 'why everyone hates me so much.'

Glen didn't deny it. There was no point denying something everyone knew was true, yet I also felt empathy coming off Glen – he didn't want to admit that reality if he could avoid it. I think he was surprised that I'd had the courage to ask, because boys didn't speak like that to each other. It was confessional in a way that laid me bare.

He looked at me for a second, tilting his head slightly like it might help him see what he was trying to describe. 'It's the way you look,' he said after a moment. Then, nodding slowly to himself as if confirming it, he repeated it.

'How?' I asked.

'It's hard to describe it,' he said. 'It's one of those things that's impossible to put into words.'

'Can you try? Maybe I can change something—'

'No,' he said, cutting me off. 'You can't. It isn't something you can change. It isn't something a person can change about themselves.'

'How do you know it's there? Does everyone see it? Maybe it's just a few—'

'*Everyone* can see it,' he said firmly. 'I know you can't see it about yourself. But everyone can see it, and I know how shitty it sounds that I can't explain something like that, but—' He paused for a moment. He was looking me in the eye, and it was kind. He could imagine how bad the thing he was saying would feel to hear, but he was saying it anyway because he wanted to help me. 'Look,' he said. 'I know it's shit, but your best bet is just to stay away from people.'

'Can you see it?' I asked.

He nodded emphatically, as if I'd finally accepted the import of what he'd described. '*Everyone* can see it,' he said.

★

I would one day read an analysis of an Italian Holocaust film in which a scholar wrote about the power of shame as an emotion. In the movie, Nazi soldiers ask a line of Jewish prisoners of war to select another prisoner for execution. It's something the soldiers do to demonstrate their absolute control. When the prisoners refuse, the commander picks someone at random and tells him to step forward. The prisoner's face betrays shame rather than fear. He is an instrument of control that has been singled out for punishment. In fact, argued the scholar, the more severe the punishment, the greater our shame at having been chosen if we do not understand the reason for the choice. Humans are social animals. Something deep in our psyches is hardwired to love the world and feel shame if we become its scapegoats.

I would come to believe that Theda's illness was tied to our experiences growing up. It was some combination of biochemistry and this type of shame we felt as children. We unsettled the world around us, and we unsettled our parents, especially our father. Yet we lacked the required understanding of the past or even the present – or perhaps more accurately, we lacked knowledge of how history was speaking through us – to make sense of why we were singled out.

Researchers would one day study the health outcomes for adults who were bullied as teenagers. If the bullying lasted longer than six months in that formative period, heart disease and chronic illness rates shoot up by middle age. It is a remarkable testament to the power of shame and the less-than-perfect division between the mind and body.

It took me a long time to understand what Glen meant. Asian kids didn't mind that I was mixed race, but whites did. Rossmoyne racists mixed epithets meant for different ethnic groups and imagined them all as one. Catalina danced like an African stereotype while conflating insults meant for Indigenous, Chinese and Vietnamese people.

What defines racism isn't who gets targeted; it is the unconscious anxieties of the more racially privileged group that targets them.

Seven

I woke up, showered and meditated before heading to the cafe where Rachel had said we should meet. It was in a row of shops a couple of suburbs over from where I was staying, and as I was early I walked down a paved path to some marshland behind the buildings to pass the time. I told myself not to pre-empt what Rachel might say. I wanted to come across as natural. My best bet at getting her to open up would be showing her that I cared about her needs more than mine.

Just before eleven, I returned to the front of the shops and found her sitting at a table about halfway down the narrow interior of the cafe. I noticed a few differences straightaway. Her hair was neatly brushed and longer. She was wearing nail polish, which wasn't something Rachel had ever worn in my presence. She'd openly expressed dismay about girly things supposedly ruling women's lives. It was part of her gender politics to eschew things like makeup and pretty dresses in general. She wasn't against them per se, but if I'd had to describe her I would have called her a tomboy, despite her feminine features and frame.

The other immediately noticeable change was her posture. Since I'd known her, Rachel had moved about the world with a lankiness that was almost teenage-like. It was playful and bouncy. I'd called her a spider-monkey sometimes, because she was prone to sitting on couches with her legs spread wide and her feet up on the cushion. Now she looked like someone had told her to imagine an invisible stack of books on her head, and to keep her knees tightly together.

As I adjusted my chair to sit down, she moved slightly and a shoal of hair shifted from her back to her shoulder. She lifted four straight fingers off the table and, keeping them straight, used them to shelve the hair back behind her again. I had a similar feeling to when I'd met my sister during one of her manic psychotic breaks. The impression was of a different person inhabiting the body of someone I knew intimately. It was uncanny.

'You've got fifteen minutes,' she said curtly.

'That's not long,' I said.

'Say what you have to. Because you're not going to see me again after this.'

'You're angry I came.'

She blinked. 'I told you not to and you did.'

'I thought we had to speak face to face,' I said, remembering how she'd been friendlier on the phone and wondering what had happened between then and now. 'We needed to do this in person.'

'No we fucking didn't,' she spat. 'You came halfway around the fucking world?'

My chest tightened. She wasn't shouting, because there were people around us, but there was an outrage in her voice that stung. 'We were planning to get married, Rachel,' I said. 'I had to know it was unsalvageable. I could let it go, but I had to come and see for myself first.'

'So you thought to show up?'

'For closure,' I said. I took a breath and felt a flash of shame because it seemed like a needy thing to say. 'I … I know that's an illusion, but there must be levels of it that are achievable. You don't have to talk about us. I would like to. But at the very least I need to be sure I've done everything I can.'

She laughed. 'So a woman tells you *not* to do something, and you think she might actually be saying *do* it?'

It felt like a trick.

'I thought you might be having some kind of breakdown,' I said, quietly enough that no one else would overhear.

'I'm not right in the head if I don't want you?'

'I thought maybe you needed me to come in person. Even if you didn't say it. All that stuff about me not being bold enough. You said I didn't believe in you. Everything was so erratic and quick. Your whole personality seemed to just suddenly change.'

An ironic smirk she'd been holding left her face, and she went quiet for a moment. I took it as encouragement. 'I don't want a perfect explanation. I don't suppose you even know how to give one, but I needed to come and try at least. You wanted to get married so sincerely, then you suddenly wanted to leave me, then you changed your mind again. Then you changed it back. It was really confusing.'

She nodded stiffly. 'I couldn't see things until I was back home,' she said. 'I was sick in Australia, but I'm much better now. I had a moment of doubting that, which is why I asked you to come. But I explained all that to you, Khin. It's not my fault if you don't get it. It certainly doesn't give you the right to turn up here when I've told you not to.'

'Did you ever really love me?' I asked. It was a dumb question. I didn't know if she would say yes, but I also knew that if she said no I wouldn't believe it. Either way, our relationship was over.

'I thought I was in love,' she said slowly, turning over some kind of feeling in her words. 'For maybe, ten … eleven months … Maybe twelve. But Khin, you should have known. You should have known I wasn't well. If you'd known the real me – the true me – you would have realised that I wasn't well and that you were the reason. You aren't the right person for me.'

'You seemed so happy.'

'I had to walk up that fucking hill every day.'

'Which hill?' As soon as I said it, I knew I'd made a mistake. There was a hill between our apartment and the supermarket where she'd worked part-time. It was symbolic in her mind. She had always said that working in an unskilled job was just part of her year abroad. But ever since her mother's visit, that idea had become suspect. Mary had seen the job as a stagnation. Rachel was now back inside her mother's narrative, in which a gap year (or two) meant downward career mobility.

'You only ever seemed happy,' I said. 'And I would have returned to America sooner. Wasn't that our original plan – just to do a year in Australia? You said another year in my country was what was best for *you*. I was following your lead.'

Her voice took on a pitying tone. 'That's the point, Khin. If you were right for me, you would have known I needed to come back regardless of what I said.'

The whole conversation felt slippery and part of me knew I wouldn't convince her of anything. I'd seen it as I sat down – she'd made up her mind. She was on a new path. I'd never seen such a dramatic change in someone close to me aside from in my sister during a psychosis, and this was something else, something I didn't have the cultural or psychological framework to understand.

'I can see you've made up your mind,' I said. 'I know now that I'm not going to get to talk to you about this in a way that helps me make sense of it. So I wonder if I can just help you understand why I came here. You don't seem to get it, so maybe that's the best I can do. Maybe that would help?'

'I don't understand,' she said bluntly.

'Can I explain?'

'Fine.' She huffed slightly and sat back in her chair. 'Go ahead. You've got a few more minutes before I have to go and meet my mother.'

I took a moment to figure out the best way of putting things I wouldn't get to explain again. 'I've been thinking', I said slowly, 'about that dream you said you had. It was a few weeks ago and you'd dreamt we had a child that you were breastfeeding. It was because of that dream that I came.' I looked at her to see if she was listening, and she was. 'It was before you broke things off again. It was evening in Australia, but you'd just woken up because it was morning here.

'You said you'd found peace with your decision asking me to come and sort things out. You talked about a place we might rent here and said you would tell your mother. I didn't know what to think of that: I'd been planning to come for four weeks by then. I'd quit my job and told the agent I was leaving the apartment in a few days. I'd packed everything up and had my plane ticket sorted. I'd assumed you had told your mother weeks ago, but you hadn't. You'd told your father but not your mother. But I didn't want to push anything, because you'd left me in Australia like you had, and I didn't understand why. So I didn't fuss about it. It worried me, but I just decided I would talk to you about things when we met up.

'Then you told me more about that dream. You said it felt like a sign that you'd made the right decision. It was like I was holding my breath.

'Then I didn't hear from you for a couple of days, and I knew something was up. You'd said that you felt safe and secure in the dream because I'd been there cuddling you from behind as you cradled our child. But now I didn't feel safe and secure, because you *weren't* calling me for some reason. You didn't explain why or tell me what you were thinking; you were just gone again.'

I stopped myself from saying anything more. I didn't want to contradict her reality. I wasn't trying to show her up as a liar. She knew all this anyway. I just wanted to remind her that it mattered.

'Then a few days later,' I said, 'you told me it was over. You told me you still loved me but that I'd hold you back. You explained it in terms of a dance performance and some kind of feeling that wasn't possible to put into words. Can you see how that was all pretty confusing from my point of view? Can you see how it made me want to come here and see if you'd talk in person?'

I had been concentrating so hard on finding the right words that I hadn't been looking at Rachel. When I did look, she had the most unusual expression on her face. It was the expression of someone who knew everything I'd just described was true but had forgotten it until hearing it again. The events weren't more than a few weeks old. It had to be a way of coping, I guessed – to forget the recent past so utterly. I had seen my father do it. I had never expected it from Rachel. She wasn't a ruthless person. But then again, neither was my father. This kind of forgetting was something a person who wasn't intentionally cruel was capable of. It made you question your own reality.

'That was part of a process,' she said haltingly. She was looking upwards with her mouth open like someone trying to do a sum in their head. 'I can see how that … might have been confusing.'

'Are you seeing that therapist?' I asked.

'She doesn't understand me,' she shot back sternly.

'Okay.'

When Rachel had initially returned to America, she'd started seeing a therapist. Ending our relationship had shocked her. She wanted to understand herself better and thought a therapist would help. Hearing this over Skype, I'd felt hopeful. Perhaps it was selfish, but the better she understood her motives the less likely it was something like this would happen again. Too many of her influences in America seemed to discourage introspection. The fact that she was now hostile to the therapist dispelled any lingering hopes I had for our conversation.

'How long will you be here?' she said, sounding a touch deflated.

'In America?'

'Are you going straight back to Australia after this?'

'I can't,' I said. 'I just can't face being there right now. I want to find a town somewhere and write. I'm still enrolled in that course online and have the savings I was going to use for our partner visa and moving here next year. It's not money I need anymore, so I figure I'll just use it and give myself a break.'

A tightness came into her voice then. 'All I have to do, Khin, is tell the police that I don't want you here and you'll have to leave.'

For years, I would wonder what happened with Rachel and me that day. I would wonder because memory is flawed, but on the surface it seems fairly clear she just changed her mind about me. She was caught between her mother's advice and her feelings about me. She didn't want me around confusing her. It would have been a trigger for doubts.

As we walked outside to say goodbye, she said she was worried about bumping into me. She would prefer if I left Albany immediately because it wasn't that big and bumping into each other wasn't a ridiculous possibility. I told her I'd stay out of her way, and if there was any place she was concerned I might go I'd give it a wide berth. I confessed that I had a month paid for in my current accommodation but would likely leave sooner now that I knew there was no chance of us rekindling things. She wasn't happy about it but said she'd cope. I told her it had been a financial decision. Nightly payments had been well out of my price range, so I'd paid a month upfront for roughly half the cost. I just needed to figure out the next part of my plan and I'd probably be gone in a fortnight.

Virginia Woolf once wrote that we don't experience emotions as they happen. It's a strange idea, but I think she meant that we notice different textures hanging together inside us around an event long after it is over. Those are textures we associate with the memory of the event and our understanding of what it was. After my teens, I'd always considered myself a good judge of character, but Rachel taught me to be less certain. The possibility of judging someone's character is an illusion, maybe. We don't know how someone's personality can change in the right circumstances, in the face of some impossible choice they see in front of them. It might be that someone has tried to defy a path that's been laid out for them while secretly believing that their only choice is to follow it.

Rachel and I reached her car. I recall the sun shining off the roofs of the other parked cars and the beep as she pressed a button on her keys. I commented on how new her car looked. I assumed it was the one she'd talked about her mother buying her as a graduation present before she'd left America some twenty months earlier.

'*Any* car is nicer than yours, Khin,' she said with a grin. It was a sudden spark of humour amid her overall dour mood. She must have caught the hint of intimacy, because she followed up by telling me she was already dating new men.

'How does that make you feel?' she said.

I told her that I didn't feel much. I wasn't jealous and she knew that about me anyway. I'd never been a possessive partner. But I could see she wasn't happy with the answer. She wanted me to be something other. Maybe it was her wish that I act in more stereotypical ways so she could do what she did next. I don't know.

I walked to my accommodation in a strange mood, sad but thinking it was a relief that I wouldn't work for another six months. I felt sorrow that I wouldn't be able to make enough sense of what had happened to communicate it to someone else in the future. That troubled me because I'd never had a story about a past lover that I wasn't comfortable sharing. And I knew this happened to people – sometimes a lover unexpectedly vanished from your life as Rachel had. But I didn't know how to make sense of it without someone suspecting we'd not been as happy as we had been. I couldn't reconcile that. If we'd been anything but a bright and deeply connected couple who loved each other's company, I would have been able to understand.

I became aware of how smooth the concrete path felt. The suburban trees were leafy and pleasant. The world around me came more into focus because I'd done the thing I needed to do.

That's all I really remember of that day.

Eight

For twelve weeks, I pretended to walk to school, when in reality I was spending my days watching fishermen down at the local river. After a while I started to go further afield. I'd never explored my city alone. A bus ticket cost seventy cents and would take me to places that I'd heard about but never killed time in alone before. I would walk the streets and sit in parks and other public places. I got a taste for being invisible in a world of adults.

The school administrators called my parents but I always got home in time to erase messages. Mum was trying to gain qualifications to work as a dental nurse, which meant she was out until about four.

During this time, I learned something I'd take into adult life – I learned how to enjoy my own company in a new environment. Once, many years earlier, my family had met a Burmese palm reader, visiting Perth on a cargo ship, who'd said I would be the adventurous child in the family. My mother hadn't believed it at the time. I had been such a tentative little boy. But during these troubled high school years, I formed a taste for unfamiliar places and the slightly off-beat solitude they offered. I wasn't bored. I felt safe. And the lives of strangers were something I enjoyed thinking about. I particularly liked wealthy suburbs because I could walk around looking at gorgeous houses and imagining a life in them that was different to my own. But it could feel like mine if I imagined myself in those living rooms.

A sort of sexual awakening gripped me that year too. I was fifteen, and most boys seemed interested in girls, but I'd kept an emotional distance. Desire was something people who weren't concerned with their safety had more mental space for. A person could apparently swallow their sexuality right down inside if it didn't feel safe to experience it, even when their hormones were supposedly running riot. Sexual interests made you a target. Boys who acted like they owned girls took their frustrations out on you if they were unsuccessful in getting them. Now with the schoolyard situation gone, I had more sexual feelings. I noticed young women with infants mostly. Especially in the more affluent suburbs, young mothers seemed to have time alone in parks and on the beach with little babies they cared for while their husbands were at work. They would have been in their twenties – an age that most teen boys would feel some attraction towards. I found them utterly gorgeous, and they were different from the bogan girls at Rossmoyne who spat and smoked and swore. Young white mothers in Perth's wealthy suburbs inspired me to masturbate for the first time.

I started two new activities during this period. The first was writing. I'd never been a big reader, and it would be years before I would learn about poetry. But I started to write about my feelings. It was mostly chaotic and not very articulate, but my writing had the strange effect of drawing emotions out of me that I didn't know I had.

Lucia Osborne-Crowley wrote that the most permanent effects of trauma come from what remains unspeakable. For boys back then, virtually every emotion aside from anger was denied in the culture. When I started to write about myself in private, I was suddenly aware of a whole range of feeling. It transformed everything. I jammed together clumsy metaphors and similes. I wrote about monsters a lot. 'Monstrous' seemed the most apt description for myself, but writing about myself as a monster in private felt very different from imagining how others saw me. I wasn't just the object of people's hatred; it seemed the most natural thing in the world to recognise that I felt pity for myself, but I hadn't been able to admit it until then. Writing about things gave them shape, and even though I abstracted emotions into words on a page, that shape made those things easier to feel in my body.

I made sure I went to classes about once or twice a week. The strategy was to skip lunch, recess, Mr Taylor's classes and last period. That way, I was never walking to or from home with other students, nor was I exposed to the social side of things during break times or sports. Attending a few classes assuaged some residual guilt I felt about my deceit.

It was on a day when I skipped final period that everything changed again. I had a place in the bushland down behind the basketball courts where I'd smoke cigarettes before going home. I would head there between seventh and eighth periods, then wait until long after the final bell before walking home.

Smoking was the other new activity I had taken up. Twenty cigarettes only cost a couple of dollars, and the Chinese-owned deli around the corner sold them to minors if you asked when no one was around. Smoking was enjoyable and rebellious, and I liked both aspects, though soon I was hooked enough to care only about the nicotine.

My smoking spot was obscured by a line of trees. It was a patch of sand with some shrubs and a few boulders. I'd never seen anyone else there before.

I had just lit up my first cigarette when Liam Murphy appeared in front of me.

'What do you want?' I said, feeling the panic rising.

'I thought we could have a chat?' he said, spitting in the sand and pulling out a packet of Winfield Blues. 'Don't worry,' he said. 'No one's coming.'

He offered me a cigarette, despite seeing one already in my hand, and when I told him no, he shrugged, flipped open the packet and took one for himself.

I looked at his face and tried to figure out if I could trust him. His greasy brown mullet hung gracefully over his neck as two crystalline blue eyes twinkled at me, the eyes of an intelligent criminal. I wanted to trust him. Most boys and girls in our school would have killed for the attention I was getting now. As long as it was genuine. As long as no one was coming behind him, in which case he was just buying time before the crowd arrived and the fight began. But there was something in his posture that made me think he didn't want to fight.

'We were just *messin*,' he said casually, as if recalling an incident on the football field. 'Can't blame the fellas. Them fuckers are taking over. It's true.'

'Who?' I said, wondering if he meant his friends were taking something over.

He looked at me as if I was dumb, and said, 'The Chinese.' Then he looked at me with one eye closed as if appraising a gem. 'You're not like the rest. They'll be running the country in ten years. Not that me and mine would be. Smart as fuck them Asians are.'

'My mum is English,' I said by rote.

'You don't have the eyes,' he said, ignoring my comment. 'You got a bit of *abo*?'

'What's that?' I said.

'Boong. Abo. You know? Justin Davies has abo in him. You'd never know it but. Where's you and yours from?'

I told him it was a country next to Thailand and he squinted. 'Spose,' he said. He paused and dragged on his cigarette. I watched him blow a smoke ring of such perfection that it made me envious. To be popular seemed like a different experience of time. The smoke ring floated across the dirty grey sand as if its underlining point was that time moved for the powerful.

'We're migrants too,' he said. 'Us Murphys. Our name is as Irish as it gets. You know Ireland?'

I told him I didn't, and also explained that I wasn't a migrant.

'No shit,' he said, tilting his head as if considering me for the first time.

I told him I only spoke English and he chuckled. Then his expression became serious. 'This place is racist as fuck,' he said. 'Perth is nothing but a glorified country town. The rest of the world doesn't give a fuck about this place. Europe is in the *northern* hemisphere. Shit, if we were even on the east coast … you seen where Perth is on a map of Australia?'

'Of course,' I said carefully, still wondering how defensive I should be.

'You gotta show them you're cool, that's all,' he said.

'Who?'

'The fellas. They need to see you like how I am right now.'

'How is that?'

'Normal,' he said. 'So they can see you're not like the kooks. They fucking hate anyone who isn't like them. Bunch of fucking racists.'

'Are they?' I said.

He tilted his head the other way. 'For an Asian, you're not that smart,' he said. 'I'll tell you what. I'll get my boys to lay off. Come back to classes. I know you been wagging – what, a few months now?'

'Maybe,' I said.

'Some of the girls were telling the fellas to lay off you,' he said. 'You know Nicole? She said something about it.'

He looked at me expectantly. Nicole Passmore was one of the pretty girls that boys talked about. I very much doubted she'd stood up for me. I'd never seen any of those girls get involved in the boys' affairs aside from idly standing by while their boyfriends harassed people.

'I reckon you might have a chance with her.'

'Bullshit,' I said.

He seemed to consider something for a moment, then nodded to himself. 'I'm having a party in two weeks. Everyone's gunna be there. It's the perfect chance to get stoned and let the lads see you're cool.'

'How would that work?' I said.

'All you gotta do is show 'em you're one of us. Taking some drugs will do that. That's all they need.'

Breaking rules was how the boys seemed to assert themselves. I knew it was true. I might succeed if Liam was at my side. The next day I tried lunch hour, and it was remarkable – no one bothered me. Even in science class, where Matt Richardson had made a ritual out of harassing me, nothing happened.

★

Liam and I shared cigarettes behind the school almost daily for the next two weeks. I mostly listened while he talked. He seemed to like talking more than listening, but that was okay with me. His brother was in juvenile detention, and Liam said he feared him because his brother was schizophrenic. Kids used the word *schizo*, he told me, but it was a medical condition with his brother. And he was violent.

I think he grew fond of me in those two weeks. 'You listen,' he said once after a few meetings. 'I can say things to you that I can't tell anyone else.'

When I asked what he meant by that, he said that everyone else in his life just talked and didn't ask questions.

I felt that I'd done something special, even though it was just how I would have engaged anyone. I'd always been more of a listener. It was how Theda and I had been – she led and I followed. I liked that role.

'I wouldn't tell them the stuff I tell you,' he said. And I believed him, though I couldn't figure out what he'd told me that was so secret. It reminded me of how Benjamin had needed me in this role when we'd been little boys. Like Liam, Benjamin knew the Shadow better than I did, but he didn't know how to talk about even the most basic of emotions if I didn't ask him the right questions. It was weird.

As much as I would come to regret my friendship with Liam, I do think he was telling the truth that day. By the second week, he asked me to his house. It was a dishevelled place on Leach Highway with a sagging front porch. Inside stank of cigarettes, and his mother barely acknowledged me. His father sat in an armchair smoking the whole time and didn't speak to me once. I felt sorry for Liam then, because

I could see that his home was pretty nasty compared to mine, despite my own parents having issues. There was a lack of kindness in the air, whereas I had my mother's kindness if nothing else. My dad was different to Liam's too. I got the sense that in this house the father had the final word. His mother was almost meek in response to her mostly silent husband's few uttered commands. I got the impression that Liam feared his father and belittled his mother because that's how his father treated her. He told her to fuck off at one point, and it shocked me, but I didn't say anything.

'I fingered Michelle Brackstone on that,' he said, pointing at the lower of two bunks in a windowless room.

'Who's that?' I said.

'She's the town bike. Total slut. Might even fuck your tiny Asian dick.'

After that, we smoked cigarettes in a backyard full of rotting couches and rusted whitegoods. There were planks of broken wood and paint cans jammed against the fence. Liam swept a perfectly formed forearm towards the scene and said, 'I don't know why my parents chuck all this crap everywhere.'

'It's not so bad,' I said.

He looked sour. 'It fucking is,' he said.

★

The night of the party, a small group of boys gave me some drugs that no one else touched. They acted like my friends, which I attributed to the work Liam had done behind the scenes, but I discovered later that those boys had been burning my hair with a lighter the whole time. While I was sucking on the can bong and they were encouraging me to inhale, one boy got his lighter up close to the back of my head. Liam was there too, so he must have seen it, but he didn't intervene.

The drugs made me feel as though the world had turned into a dream, and when we returned to the backyard (they'd fed me the drugs down the road, away from the main house), the party was in full swing with over a hundred people. Iron Maiden was playing from speakers jammed in the living room windows. Owen Brady dragged me to the side fence and punched me several times while another boy watched. I managed to stagger away, but Brad McCormick was performing for a group of kids halfway down the driveway and pulled me into the middle of the circle and filled his mouth with beer before spitting it in my face. The crowd was delighted.

I didn't see Liam until I was making my way out. He was talking to two girls in the driveway, and I didn't have time to stop because Owen Brady was yelling at me from behind to get my arse back into the party. I turned to see him punching the air and marching towards me with a massive grin. He caught up with me and smashed me four or five times in the side of my head as I tried to get away. I saw Liam laughing and slapping his knee as the two girls watched on like it was a distraction from the thing they'd been talking about beforehand.

★

A couple of months later, the school showed my parents a list that apparently proved I'd been absent from classes for six months straight. The vice principal said I was not to come back to school the following year because year eleven wasn't compulsory and they didn't want me returning.

'All they care about is how good their tertiary entry scores are in the local paper,' Mum said as we were leaving. 'And that's thanks to all those Asian students they have.'

It was true. One thing I noticed about the school was that the ratio of Asians to whites was different in the upper grades. White bogans dropped out and Asian kids stayed on. Many of the boys who'd been the worst to me would probably stop going to school after this year too, but I would never know.

As we passed a placard outside the front entrance, I saw the school motto embossed on bricks: *Success Nourishes Hope*. It didn't even make sense, I realised. It should have been the other way around because hope was what nourished success, not the reverse. That was the last time I ever entered Rossmoyne Senior High School grounds.

73

Nine

The hostel dormitory I'd stayed in back in New York City was more expensive than the room I had to myself in Albany. The room was half the price of anything else in the country, as far as I could tell. There was a coal town in Philadelphia and a college town in Vermont I had thought about going to – both looked appealing but well beyond what I could afford.

By mid-afternoon, I had found one hotel south of the Mason-Dixon Line, in a town called Savannah, that was affordable. It was still more expensive than my current place, but only by a couple of hundred dollars if I paid by the month. The thing that worried me was some online reviews mentioning gun violence nearby.

An email from Rachel arrived just before dinnertime. She was angry again: *What right do you have to be in my city? My father didn't want to go to work today because he was so afraid of someone that his daughter didn't want in her city. Mom is going to talk to a lawyer who's a family friend to see what we can do.*

I emailed back immediately saying that I only needed some time. I reminded her that I wasn't in a great financial situation and suggested she not contact me if she didn't want to talk or see me. She wrote back half an hour later in a different tone, frazzled and confused, telling me it was okay.

I spent most of the next morning online, getting a bit neurotic. Savannah looked like a singer-songwriter's town – that was good because I could make friends that way. Open mic events were how I'd made friends in strange cities earlier in my life. Bus tickets to Savannah weren't cheap, though. I hadn't bargained on the American South either, so I needed time to think about it.

I went to the grocery store around midday to clear my head, meaning to make a firm decision once I got back. When I returned, I entered through the back door via the downstairs kitchen, and there was a tall shaggy man cooking something on the stove. He was the first guest I'd seen since arriving, and I introduced myself. He told me that he was an itinerant carpenter who worked Albany in the summer, and then he told me about the police who'd been there while I was out.

'They just left,' he said. 'I think they were looking for you.' He squinted and looked at me, then pointed past the main downstairs area to the front door. 'Three of them in uniform, right there, up on the landing.'

'What did they want?' I asked.

'Didn't say,' he said unconvincingly. 'I figured it was you when you came in. Said they were looking for a darker guy, Asian, you know? But with an Australian accent. Figured there couldn't be many folks around here like that.'

'Did you call the manager?' I asked anxiously.

He must have noted the anxiety in my voice because he looked apologetic. 'You're fine,' he said. 'I can tell that now. But *three* of them, you know, right? Out there on the deck in uniform asking about a guest. I had to call her.'

I thanked him and went upstairs.

The sensation I had is difficult to describe. I could barely think and my heart was hammering. Ever since Rachel had first become irate on a Skype call, I'd known she was inclined to make threats. When she'd told me to be a 'fucking man', she'd also torn things off her bedroom wall and thrown them at the computer screen. I didn't seem to know her anymore. Eberhardt had encouraged me to come but warned me to be careful. I had been, but when I thought about the implications of an older foreign brown man coming to see a beautiful young white woman who'd told him not to visit, I wondered if Eberhardt and I had both made a mistake. Suddenly, it seemed particularly likely that I had. Drawing the ire of the local authorities would be easy. Rachel was right – all she needed to do was call them.

I spent a couple of hours completely unsure of what to do. I looked up things on the internet. Some web pages suggested contacting a lawyer. I knew I couldn't afford that. Rachel obviously wanted to disavow me in some way, and it was probably related to her networks and reputation here. None of her friends knew me. Her family barely knew me. Rachel and I had had our relationship away from the people she was closest to. So what would the cops think when she told them I'd travelled across the globe to see her against her wishes? I had no one to vouch for me. 'A darker guy, Asian' – what did that imply? Dangerous, prone to resentment, unreasonable?

An old news story about an active shooter at Virginia Tech snuck into my mind. I'd read it a few years earlier and stereotypes about Asian men had risen up in my thoughts. I remembered how the boys I'd grown up with had viewed the Asian boys: feminine and objectively undesirable. It was easy to imagine the shooter was a 'repressed Asian male', desperate to fit in and confused about why he couldn't catch much validation, especially from white women. The story lingered in my mind along with a lot of other worries.

Eventually, I left the house and headed for the police station across the road.

★

The station was small inside, with a row of plastic chairs against one wall. A young woman in a blue uniform addressed me from behind the counter. I told her that policemen had come looking for me and that I was pretty sure it was about my ex.

'Where do you live?' she said, smiling.

Her friendliness caught me off guard. I was also unsure of my exact address. 'It's here,' I said. 'On this intersection.'

She looked at me for a moment, her bright manner fading slightly.

'I'm sorry,' I said. 'I've only just moved to Albany. I'm from Australia.' I did my best to mime a description of where my B & B was in relation to the police station.

'You mean kitty-corner?' she said after a moment, recognition entering her eyes.

'Yes,' I said, unscrambling the American slang term.

She glanced at a male officer, snowed under with paperwork at one of the desks behind her. Apart from the two of them, the station was empty. The office space was large, with lots of unattended computers. 'Barry?' she said.

The man looked up.

'Do you remember that guy we tried to serve across the road?' she said.

The word *serve* lodged in my mind.

'On the corner here,' she insisted.

Barry – a middle-aged man with a resigned face – nodded slowly, extracting himself from the task in front of him. He reached for a pile of papers and pulled some loose. The policewoman walked away from the counter, collected the papers, returned and smiled as she put them on the counter between us. She was in her late twenties and there was a sturdiness about her. Her hands were chapped and irritated like they'd been scrubbed too many times.

'It's just this,' she said, before turning back to the man at the desk. 'Barry,' she said. 'I can serve these, right? I mean, do I get him to sign the logbook?'

The man confirmed I'd need to sign.

When she turned back to me, I asked about the meaning of the word 'served'.

'This is from the family court,' she said, as if that explained everything. 'The date you have to appear will be on the back.'

'Appear?' I said.

She nodded. 'In family court.'

'What for?'

She patted the papers. 'It's all in there. This is only a police matter if you don't appear in court on that date.' She flipped some pages. 'Yes, your date is in a month. The judge has issued a temporary order of protection until then. You have to keep your distance from the person who lodged it.'

She must have seen the anxiety on my face because she added, 'Don't worry, you're not in any trouble with us. This is a *family* court matter. Your only issue here is if you break that temporary protection order or don't turn up.'

I failed to see how I wasn't in trouble with the police. Their handing me official documents demanding my appearance in court seemed like trouble. I smiled unconvincingly.

'Look,' she said. 'We just serve these. They're not actually anything to do with us.'

I had no idea what she meant. Stalking was a crime and everyone knew that. I reached for the papers, and she stopped me short. 'You need to sign first,' she said, lifting up a heavy logbook.

I signed, and after that, she told me that if there was anything I didn't understand I could come back and she would explain what she could. I thanked her and returned to my room.

★

In the room, I cocooned in the attic's dim lamplight and tried to make sense of the document. I was labelled the *respondent* in the first pages and Rachel was the *petitioner*. Her handwritten statement explaining her reasons for applying to the court was on the second page. She hadn't given any context, and whether we'd actually been in a committed relationship was unclear. The statement didn't mention that we'd had plans to marry or that she had left me unexpectedly in Australia, had changed her mind and asked me to come to the US and then changed it back again. It said that I had refused to leave Albany and had been 'agitated' in our meeting at the cafe. I didn't understand it. Was my assertion that I *would* be leaving Albany (soon) somehow irrelevant if I didn't do it immediately? Was something I'd said in the cafe 'agitated'? What was the meaning of that word when used in a legal context?

The most immediately troubling page was the last one. It was titled 'Order of Protection' and outlined nine places I wasn't allowed to go near. It also stipulated that I wasn't allowed to get near Rachel in person nor communicate with her in any way.

An hour later, I was back in the police station trying to explain to the officer that I didn't know where any of the nine places were.

'It says I'm not allowed within a certain distance of them,' I said. 'But what if I accidentally go past one and don't realise it?'

She swivelled the papers around to better read them. They were described in a way that Rachel would know where they were but I wouldn't:

- The petitioner's home
- The petitioner's workplace
- The petitioner's school
- The petitioner's mother's home and workplace
- The petitioner's father's home and workplace
- The petitioner's brother's home and school

Maybe I was being paranoid, but Albany was a small place. Back in Perth, Rachel had described it as a city of a million people. I'd only just learned the real number was a hundred thousand. Albany was one in a cluster of small cities that altogether amounted to roughly a million people. I was probably close to the nine places listed on the order.

'Well,' the policewoman said, 'just stay away from the places you *do* know.'

'What would happen if she said I'd broken this?'

She frowned slightly. 'If you did that, it would become a criminal matter.'

I tried to make sense of that response. 'I don't mean I *would* break it,' I said. 'I guess I mean what would happen if she saw me walking down the street and *decided* I'd broken it? Even if I'd never meant to do anything wrong, would I be in trouble?'

The policewoman seemed genuinely not to understand the question. I wondered again if I was being paranoid. Maybe such a scenario was far-fetched, but too many things had gone wrong for me not to be worried another might go badly.

'As I said,' she told me, 'there are only two ways you can get in trouble with us: if you don't appear in court on the specified date, or if you break this order.'

I thanked her and left.

There was a college down a nearby road. I had no idea if it was her brother's school. Last time we'd spoken on the phone, Rachel had said that universities weren't taking new enrolments at this time of year, so the instruction saying I needed to avoid her school was confusing. Had Rachel found a way of enrolling anyway?

As I walked up the stairs to my attic room, I couldn't stop thinking about a Louis Theroux documentary. Theroux had interviewed a weedy guy in a Florida jail who said he was innocent. He hadn't had his day in court yet, but a judge had put him in a crowded jail cell with men twice his size while he awaited trial. He said they were threatening to rape him. He told Theroux that his only crime had been driving without a licence, a claim I'd been sceptical of but Rachel had told me could be genuine. She'd said the American incarceration system was a capitalist endeavour, and courts were often extremely quick to jail people. Could that be true? And if so, how could Rachel do something like that to me? I was a man she'd professed to love for the last year and a half. Did she think I deserved to be jailed and potentially beaten up or raped? No one cared about men getting raped in jail – that was another conversation we'd had after watching that documentary. Once in the system, they were considered second-class citizens, and not even the media made a fuss about how regular rapes and murders were. I found it hard to reconcile all of this with the social-justice-minded person I'd admired so deeply and loved. She was against this kind of authoritarianism. She thought jails and prisons were racist. She thought the entire criminal justice system was biased and had even ranted about how unfair it was that the US treated foreign entrants so suspiciously. 'Why should I have the right to reside in America just because I was born there?' she'd said once. I'd found her assertion idealistic, but I'd admired it too. Maybe that was the problem – ideals often go untested. It feels one way to say something and quite different when you're called upon to hold to it.

I re-read some of the other pages in the document. There were short questions on one page that elicited information about my criminal history. Rachel had written that I'd once been convicted of 'dangerous and reckless driving'. It wasn't true – I'd once blown a touch over the limit and lost my licence, but it was considered a traffic offence. I knew that because I'd looked into it at her behest when we were considering factors that could get in the way of me entering the country. How did the court verify things like that? Would they just take her word? She knew it wasn't a criminal offence, certainly not one with the label 'dangerous and reckless driving' – she'd just made that up. She was bending the truth. How far was she willing to bend it to get what she wanted? She wanted me out of Albany *yesterday* as opposed to a fortnight from now. She must have called all the B & Bs in Albany to find out where I was staying. I hadn't told her. It didn't seem paranoid to imagine her using the restraining order to get me booted out of the country altogether. Maybe that was what she wanted most – for me to be gone from the northern hemisphere so she could pretend I'd never existed.

I realised something else in her statement was bad for me too. My B & B was too close to her mother's house. It was the only place on the list that I knew the location of, and it was about two miles away. I knew the address because it had been on the paperwork for our de facto partner visa in Australia. I'd noticed how close it was to the B & B when booking online from Australia, but it hadn't seemed something to worry about then. Besides, this was the only place I could afford. It had seemed serendipitous if anything. Because if things had worked out between us, I would have been close enough to walk over to visit Rachel while we figured out our next move together.

I began speculating about how I might defend my version of the story to strangers. I could show a judge my B & B's prices relative to those of other B & Bs, but they would need to see my bank details to confirm I'd really had no other choice. It was unlikely they would ask. I could explain the context Rachel had left out of her statement. But would that be considered relevant? When did the law think a bumbling attempt at saving a relationship crossed over into suspicious behaviour? The benefit of the doubt was what people in my situation needed more than anything. I didn't feel like I had the benefit of anyone's doubt. No one here could vouch for me except Rachel.

Ten

Theda had reached the end of her rope at her selective school in the city and asked our mother to let her move to Rossmoyne High. I didn't think to warn her about the bullying or the racism. It never occurred to me that she would share my fate. I was still denying that the colour of my skin had been a factor.

My new school was in Applecross, a few suburbs over from Rossmoyne. It wasn't in our catchment zone, but we'd told a little lie to get me in. The schoolyard wasn't mired in racial tensions. The few Asian kids mixed with white kids and no one mentioned it. Casual bigotry got voiced from time to time but only against the foreign exchange students from Japan.

Despite how much safer my new school was for me, I quickly identified the roughest group of white boys I could and befriended them. After a year of not seeing much bullying, I ditched the rough boys and repeated Year 11. I even thought about going to university. I might not have done my tertiary entrance exam had it not been for a drama teacher. He'd told me I was talented and could study acting.

My homeroom teacher ridiculed this idea as she handed over the paperwork for doing Year 12. 'Why would you bother?' she said, encouraging the class to laugh along with her. I suppose she had no idea that my classroom behaviour until then had been about ensuring my physical safety. Why would she? They didn't teach women that equation about boys. My own mother didn't understand it, so why would she?

During my first year at the new school, Theda had troubles with bullies at Rossmoyne. She'd struggled with friends at her selective school, but Rossmoyne was another level. People left rubbish in her backpack and started rumours. As with me, the number of kids doing it was abnormal. Both genders were involved in harassing her, and they routinely threatened violence. There was an incident where she, too, was invited to a party as the entertainment without knowing it. A group of girls pushed her into a swimming pool. The whole thing was planned, just as Liam's party had been a year earlier.

I'm sorry to say that I was only vaguely paying attention. But unlike me, Theda told our mother. It was springtime when Mum went into Rossmoyne for a parent–teacher night. Theda had been missing classes due to 'sickness' – sickness our father said was in her head.

We stayed in the car as our mother went in to talk to Mrs Woods, the deputy principal.

'One of my teachers thinks it's racism,' Theda said to me.

I asked if she knew what racism meant, because the word troubled me.

'It's when people hate you for the colour of your skin,' she said.

'I know that's what it kinda means,' I said. 'It's weird. It's one of those words – people act like it's so important when it comes up, but I never figured out how to use it.'

She told me that she wasn't sure either. 'I don't know if it applies to us,' she said. 'Because we're not African.'

'How dark does your skin have to be before it's racism?'

She furrowed her brow. 'Maybe Dad's colour,' she said. 'Mum says he gets mistaken for an Aborigine sometimes.'

'Do they get racism?' I said.

'I'm not sure. I think so.'

I thought of our father's skin. It was the colour of damp soil. Dad wasn't African, but most Asians were much lighter skinned than him. We didn't have any African people in Perth as far as I knew. I knew that the word was significant for them because I'd heard it in American movies. In primary school we learned that what Hitler did to the Jews was racism, but the Jews were *white.* The whole thing was confusing, but I had more pressing things to worry about. I think something inside Theda and me also resisted using the word to describe our experiences because we worried we might be stealing it from African American people.

We agreed tacitly that the word 'racism' might possibly apply to our father but definitely not to us. He also had an accent, which added something. His legs were slightly bandy and his frame was different to a white man's. He was short.

When our mother returned to the car, she was furious. She told us that Mrs Woods had said that Theda couldn't be experiencing bullying because Rossmoyne had an anti-bullying policy, which Mrs Woods had verified by pointing at a poster on her office wall. She told Mum that Theda must be lying. Our mother said Mrs Woods was a bitch. That was thrilling because Mum never swore.

During that year, Mum went into Rossmoyne High several more times. Eventually, one of the teachers came forward and confirmed the bullying. That teacher confronted some of the ringleaders. Theda was already a mess, though. Just being a teenager was difficult enough. Our father barely spoke to us, but when he did he continued to insist we weren't Asian enough. Our mum wanted us to be like kids from a little English village of the type she'd grown up in. The kids who bullied us at school said we weren't Aussie enough. It felt like betraying everyone, including the bullies. Theda and I drew too much attention, and surely that was ultimately on us. Even at my new school, I was constantly answering the same questions about where I was 'really' from, and I never felt comfortable with any particular answer. I felt I was unknowable in some way that others weren't, and that weirdly made everything I did feel like an act. I imagine Theda was having a similar experience.

★

I befriended a boy called Quin in Year 12 who lived just across the road from school. After classes each day, I would go to his house to smoke cigarettes. Quin said I was a good listener, just like Liam had. He said he was comfortable talking about his feelings with me. By then, I was used to that role and liked it. I recognised that I operated as a sort of proxy girlfriend. Quin had a cooler friend called Dylan who filled the roles I couldn't. Dylan had finished high school two years earlier and was dating a girl in our year called Angela. Angela was the first 'pretty' girl that I'd ever known. She was petite, skinny and blonde, and she came to Quin's for cigarettes after school too.

One night, when I was out with the three of them, I saw something that would play on my mind in the coming years, as I tried to make sense of my hometown's culture and what it had done to Theda and me. It was one of the few incidents of racial bullying I witnessed from the other side, although, like Theda and me, the victim was someone who thought he could mix with white kids.

I was at a party in Ardross, a reasonably wealthy suburb next to Applecross. Quin, Dylan, Angela and I had all taken LSD when we arrived. A squelchy boy called Jared was with us too. He was ugly and a bit mean, but never gave me any trouble. The party was hosted by some boys from an expensive Catholic boys' school whose parents lived in the countryside. It was an old brick place from the '70s, and the partygoers were in plastic chairs on the back patio when we arrived. There were only about fifteen people, none of whom I recognised. I got shuffled to the least desirable chair next to an Indian boy.

'I'm Elliot,' he said. 'You're Asian too!'

I gave him my usual line about being the son of an Englishwoman. We shook hands and, despite myself, I felt warmly towards him. He was trying so hard. He had about him the same softness that Theda and I had, and he was trying to negotiate a world of swear words and put-down humour.

As conversation swirled, it soon became apparent that Elliot had been invited to the gathering as a joke. I didn't know any people from private schools, but obviously they had some of the same tricks.

Elliot had fallen for the trap Theda and I had. I think he knew it too. It was strange to see from the outside. His clumsy extroversion seemed like an attempt to be okay with it, because he so desperately wanted to be there. The boys who'd invited him, on the other hand, were thrilled by anything he did because it drew him deeper into their trap.

'You're the man, Elliot!' they shouted.

'Keep it coming, Elliot!'

'Don't stop now, Elliot!'

Elliot, recognising that he was being given a role, was letting himself be egged on. He was attempting jokes, but they were too clean. He lifted his cup in salute and then fell off his chair. It was not too different from the dumb act some girls put on around popular boys. I watched him get drunk without getting involved. Then, to my relief, he stumbled off into the dark recesses of the backyard to be ill.

I don't know how much time passed.

They brought his unconscious body back.

One boy had him under the arms and the other had his feet. A third was bouncing around like a terrier. Kids on the patio around me started shouting, and the terrier-like boy yelled at us to get some sheets. They took Elliot over to the Hills hoist, which was a good staging area because it caught enough light from the patio to be seen but was separate from the onlookers.

Teen bullying involving groups is a ritual. Like all rituals, the group seeks collective transformation. For teenagers, spectacles that involve scapegoats are perfect for creating a sense of unity among the onlookers, as they collectively project their own anxieties onto the person who is objectified and destroyed.

Jared was beside me, looking on eagerly. Quin and Angela stayed put. A lot of the other boys got up from their chairs to go and join in. Dylan wasn't there because he'd disappeared inside the house upon our arrival. Some girl had recognised him and ushered him away, much to Angela's barely hidden resentment.

I remember the LSD that night wasn't overwhelming. I felt detached and calm.

When someone from the Hills hoist called for us to get a razor, Quin stared down at the concrete and ignored them. Jared began looking hopefully between the Hills hoist and the house's back door.

'Don't be pussies!' someone called.

Quin raised his beer and smiled. 'I hate it when this happens,' he whispered to me. 'They did the same to Tom Spencer last week.'

'Who?' I said.

'Rory and Marcus. They got him stoned.'

Jared laughed through a mouthful of beer and said Tom Spencer was a faggot. Quin ignored him and adjusted his chair to start telling me the story. I knew Tom. Once, a teacher had asked him to read a passage aloud in class and he'd rushed to the toilet. I was pretty sure he couldn't read.

Just then, a cheer erupted at the Hills hoist because someone had bypassed us and got bedsheets from inside. They were big white ones, and the group had succeeded in stringing Elliot's dark brown body from one of the metallic arms of the Hills hoist. His trousers were gone, and he had no top. Black skin shone in the moonlight, surrounded by fifteen or so white faces, grinning at how they were about to transform themselves.

'Tom spewed,' Quin said. 'They stuffed him into a shopping trolley. You know that hill from the school down to Riseley Street? They let the trolley roll down it into the intersection with him inside. It was late, so there weren't many cars. But they played Russian roulette with him.'

'I'm going inside,' said Angela.

'Tom Spencer is a dickhead,' Jared said.

Quin looked at him. 'I don't want to see it. If that's what they want, power to them. But I'd rather not see.'

Time moves unevenly with LSD. I know that Quin was keen to leave as the commotion by the Hills hoist escalated. More people arrived and the night was still young, but he meant it about not wanting to see. I might have stayed just because I was so numb to things like that, but I was glad our group leader was making a decision. He went inside to look for Angela. The people at the Hills hoist took Elliot's unconscious body up by the side of the house and then vanished with it, presumably to take him into the front garden.

I was still thinking of it as a small gathering, but when Quin returned with Angela some time later, and we headed into the front yard to leave, there were a couple of hundred kids stopped at the spectacle of Elliot on the verandah. By this stage he was on his feet and staggering around. He was trying to knock on the front door, and the crowd had formed a thick half-moon around him. He was missing chunks of hair. He had vomit down one arm and an eyebrow gone.

We didn't join the audience, but I could see clearly. Elliot swayed and lifted one arm compliantly as someone from the crowd shouted, 'Nigger-lips!'

'Keep knocking, Vijay!' a voice yelled.

'Who's Vijay?' I asked Quin. 'I thought his name was Elliot?'

'Must be his Indian name,' Quin said. 'You know how lots of Asians do that?'

I heard a crunch like a beer bottle caught under a car tire. A moment later, a boy came up to our little group and offered an open egg carton to Angela. She turned him down, and the boy moved on, and I realised that the sound had been an egg shattering against the bricks. They were throwing them at him.

Things got fuzzy then. We looked for Dylan and couldn't find him. Quin said he'd go back into the house for one last look. Angela and I ended up together near the curb, smoking cigarettes. I'd never had a conversation with Angela before. She tolerated me because Quin did, but we didn't have anything to say. Now she seemed angry.

'Fucking idiot,' she said.

'Who?'

'That Elliot guy. I mean, who comes to a party where people don't like them? Those boys probably treat him like shit at school. Surely he'd have known this would happen. It's his own fault. He should never have got so drunk.'

I looked at her for a moment. She troubled me. A girl like Angela would have never experienced anything like broad social rejection. She was subordinate to the likes of Dylan and Quin, but she certainly wasn't hated. She had no idea why someone would come to a place that might be dangerous because *everywhere* felt like somewhere you didn't belong. When that was your reality, your instincts got muddled and you hoped beyond rational thought that an invitation somewhere might finally be what you'd always needed to become normal. She took belonging for granted. She couldn't even see that it mattered. And yet if Elliot had been a white girl surrounded by a braying crowd wanting to see her stripped of all dignity, already stripped of clothes and bodily autonomy and too drunk to know it, Angela would have been outraged. Ironically, a girl like Angela could have stopped the ritual. People paid attention when pretty white girls intervened in matters. We might have all been living in a patriarchy, but a girl like Angela had power that Elliot, me and probably even Jared didn't have.

Instead, she said, 'He's gunna regret it in the morning.' And she lit a cigarette.

I mostly remember fragments after that. The ringleaders took Elliot off the verandah and a few key tormentors brought him to the tree near the curb. They put him on his knees and forced him to pose like a dog while taking photos. They were shoving dry leaves in his ears and trying to get him to eat dirt.

'That's polaroid,' Angela said. 'Melissa has a camera like that she got for her birthday. It's old technology, but it's cool.'

★

By the time I was out of school, I had a healthy hatred for the city I lived in. In years to come, many other things would confirm my suspicion that people like Theda and me didn't belong there. A few months after witnessing Elliot's humiliation, a boy I'd known at Rossmoyne attacked me. It was at a bus stop. He saw me and remembered I was a target, so he came at me. The fight was simple. A crowd gathered to watch, and I pushed through adrenaline and fear. I didn't get hurt, but I was relieved when a bus driver broke it up.

The next day, my attacker turned up at my house with another boy (he must have looked up my address in the phone book – we were the only 'Myints' in Perth). The whole thing ended with Dad speaking to the boy's mother over the phone. She confided that her son had attacked me at the bus stop after appearing in court on rape charges laid by his sister against him.

A week after that, two boys who'd witnessed the fight with the sister-rapist attacked me. It was at the same bus station. I had never met them, but I guess they thought I made a good victim. A bus driver stopped that one too, but I didn't come away unscathed. I had blood coating my chin and shirt when I got home, and my mother took me to the police station.

A policewoman said I could press charges but that the boys (Quin had told me their names) were part of a gang who might target me for it.

The next day, a policeman came to the bus stop and demanded I empty my backpack. I suppose it's because I was a brown kid smoking a cigarette. Or maybe the policewoman from the station had sent him there.

A week later, I narrowly avoided another fight in the city, when a man in his thirties followed me out of a train station.

When I was seventeen, my first girlfriend – a sweet Italian girl from Hope Valley – took me to meet her father, who challenged me to a fistfight because he didn't want his daughter dating an Asian. I remember she drove her car into him so he couldn't get to me. We'd not even spoken to each other and he was coming around the bonnet to try to rip me out of the passenger seat.

The thing about racism's effect on you is that it doesn't feel like it's coming from a single attacker. It feels like an overwhelming message from many people and places that there is something wrong with you and you deserve bad things.

I got into university. It showed me a different side of Perth, particularly because I started an arts degree. Young men and women around me wanted to express themselves. They had a different way of dressing to the people I'd grown up with. They bought clothes from op-shops and mixed them in a specific manner that baffled me. I quickly found that talking about my experiences made people uncomfortable.

At university, hip white students talked about intertextuality and postmodernism. Lecturers talked about how we all needed to unlearn our cultural programming. They said our normality was, in fact, just socially constructed. *Everything* was socially constructed. Somehow the way they taught it made me feel simultaneously patronised and misunderstood – as someone who'd come to feel that everything I did was an act, I had never really believed in the Truth of normality; but as a victim of violence and ostracism, I found the language used to deconstruct 'normality' alienating and elitist. All the lecturers were white, upper-class and pretentious in my estimation.

I wrote an essay arguing that reality itself was socially constructed and got a zero. I had no idea what scholarly texts were. But it didn't take much for me to assume university was simply an extension of high school's delusions – full of grandeur and mottos that really signified nothing. I'd come to university wanting to be an actor because it seemed one of the few ways to explore emotional complexity with some help and formal guidance, but the acting course was poorly taught and the cultural studies units forced upon us didn't mention masculinity or the emotional poverty of men, ideas that would have engaged and resonated with me. I only saw students who'd had very different childhoods. They were white and many of them were privately educated, and they talked about shared experiences that I couldn't grasp. I might have tried to get into the performing arts academy instead, but part of me knew acting was probably out of the question because there weren't roles for Asian-looking people. Asian people weren't in plays or on screens.

In the end, I stopped going to classes and started drinking heavily. I was living on Austudy, in a one-bedroom apartment, and I didn't have close friendships.

I attempted suicide twice that year.

Mum finally found a job in the government dental hospital and took out a mortgage on a house she moved into with Theda. I didn't want to live with them because of Mum's depression. I loved my mother and sister, but I needed some distance from our family as I transitioned into adulthood.

★

The suicide attempts saved my life in the end. They forced me to leave Perth. I vowed I would never return, and it was the best thing I could have done. I lived in inner-city Melbourne for four years and it opened my mind to a better world. The masculinity was less aggressive and more open to feminine qualities. The attitudes weren't racist and homo-phobic. I learned how to work at an unskilled job with pride, and it stirred a sense of optimism.

After high school, Theda became emotionally opaque. She stayed in Perth and tried to get the validation she'd always craved. We had great conversations about our thoughts and feelings when we talked on the phone. But when I visited Perth each year around Christmas time, I worried about what I saw in her. She was deeply dissociated from her emotions – especially anger. She, too, seemed to feel that being in the world was an act, but she'd embraced it and was trying to succeed at it, whereas I'd ultimately rejected it and begun to care less about what people thought I should be. Her people-pleasing behaviour seemed false and uptight. Some of her friends even mentioned it. They were new friends. High school was over and she had better people around her, but they had no idea about my sister. I'm sure they were anti-racist in their stated views, but to them this meant professing colour blindness. They couldn't recognise how racial difference might deeply affect a half-Asian Australian who'd been born ahead of her city's ability to adapt.

Developmental trauma is about an identity formed by adolescent experiences that leads a person to believe they're defective and ultimately worthless. It happens when a person develops their sense of self amid constant messages that they're incomplete, faulty or unworthy of love for some intrinsic reason. Lucia Osborne-Crowley puts it well when she describes how trauma destabilises a personality. She cites research that indicates how traumatic events mean we often become people pleasers to avoid being looked at too closely: 'We conceal ourselves because we are so ashamed that if we are seen, the rotten core will be seen too.'

My mother once told me privately that she could see why people sometimes said Theda was fake. Mum and I both knew the real Theda, but she didn't let anyone else see her properly.

'I'm afraid', she told our mother when she made some friends at university, 'that I'll say something stupid and make them hate me. They'll see what's horrible about me and gang up on me.' She pleaded with our mother to listen in on her phone conversations from another line so if she said something wrong Mum could pretend to need her in the kitchen.

When I think back on this, it breaks my heart. I knew my sister as a child before the self-protective shell formed around her. There is a photo of us that captures how she was back then. She's taller than me by about a foot, and we've been playing dress-ups. I have on a silly hat and a white toga that she's dressed me in. We're walking towards whoever took the photo, but I'm looking up at her, enthralled by her face, while she stares down the barrel of the lens. She's wearing a black T-shirt that's too big for her. We're darker-skinned as children than we would be as adults – less capable of potentially passing as white – and she has a fringe that comes down below her chin. I'm holding her hand.

Her expression betrays such certainty about who she is in the world. She's not performing, even though we're playing some kind of game. She knows where she belongs. If anyone looks less sure of themself, it's me.

By our twenties, our roles had somehow reversed. In short, I was dealing with developmental trauma one way, and Theda was dealing with it in another. My method involved dismissing institutions and people who were 'mainstream' (my friends tended to be outsiders), while Theda's way was to seek institutional validation and friends who would be considered normal by anyone's standards.

Whenever I saw Theda in person, visiting Perth from a different life I was creating for myself across the Nullarbor, it seemed to me that she was trapped. She was trying to be invisible by performing what she thought was expected. She modulated her speech and never said a bad word about anyone. Being 'normal' was essential to her survival strategy, whereas I privately ridiculed the idea of normality and felt superior to it. My strategy wasn't exactly brimming with nuance, but it protected me.

After her arts degree, Theda got into a broadcast journalism course at the performing arts academy and started aiming at a career in TV. It was an elite course that only took a handful of students. It prided itself on a tough-love approach because the industry it was training people for was so cutthroat.

I remember a phone call from Theda in the early 2000s. A lecturer had told an Indian student in her class that Australian audiences wouldn't accept his dark skin, so he should focus on radio instead of television.

'They say I'm different to him,' she said. 'That I'm ethnically ambiguous enough to still make it.'

I could hear how badly she was affected. The lecturer's comment wasn't aimed at her, but it had triggered an anxiety that something inside her was dirty, just as she'd always suspected. And it suggested that hiding that *thing* would require ever more vigilant effort. We were in the Pauline Hanson period that year, and the future senator had just warned Australia that it was being swamped by Asians. Over in Melbourne's inner city, people were saying that Hanson was a racist. It was easy for white people to talk. I knew what Theda knew. I knew Hanson was just saying what others had said our whole lives – that we weren't acceptable if our Asian aspects shone through too much. I didn't even think of that as racism; it was reality. I couldn't hide my skin or name, so I hid things *associated* with brown skin and Asian features – certain gender traits, specific emotions, tastes, *tells*. I had to be careful because there was something putrid inside us Myints, and while people sometimes overlooked it, it was there if we didn't work hard enough to obscure it.

For Theda, the terror of being found out was amplified by the career she had chosen to pursue. She wanted to be a TV journalist because she was smart as a whip and driven by social-justice ideals. Such a public job had the potential to be an antidote to shame, but it was also risky. If a viewing public accepted her it would validate her beyond belief. But if it didn't, the rejection would be further proof of that disgusting thing inside. What if her vigilance faltered on camera and a whole nation saw it and then rejected her? She wouldn't survive that.

Despite our wonderful long phone conversations on opposite coasts, whenever I visited in person I sensed her terror. I also felt there was a deep sadness that she was trying to pretend wasn't there. I wanted her to face it. I was sure it was the same sadness as mine. I knew it was shame, but I had no idea how to talk about it with her.

Part Two

Eleven

A series of questions on the fourth page of the court papers reminded me of an American spectre:

1. Did the incident involve a gun?
2. Has the respondent ever threatened you or your family members with a gun?
3. Does the respondent own a gun?
4. Does the respondent have a permit for a gun?

The last thing I could imagine was how guns might relate to what had happened between Rachel and me. But when guns are everywhere, do breakups have different unspoken rules? Was my coming to the US an over-the-line act, even if it wouldn't have been if we were in Australia?

I flipped over to the second page. A list of potential offences:

1. sexual abuse;
2. harassment;
3. strangulation;
4. forcible touching;
5. aggravated harassment;
6. stalking;
7. attempted assault;
8. criminal obstruction of breathing and circulation.

Rachel had circled number six. Being jammed between *aggravated harassment* and *attempted assault* on a list led by *sexual abuse* certainly undermined my confidence. That was a list no one wanted to be on.

★

The following day, I made several phone calls. The first was to my mother, who was furious with Rachel's family.

'What sort of people do this?' she said.

'Rachel isn't thinking straight,' I said. 'And her mother is a devil in her ear.'

'Don't make excuses. I never liked her, Khin. She's not a warm person.'

I wasn't sure I believed it, but Rachel had never been likeable according to Mum. After Rachel's sudden decision to leave me, Mum had offered to take her to the airport and went to our apartment to collect her. Rachel behaved with a flippancy Mum didn't like – she offered Mum a half-used bottle of hand cream as a 'thank-you-for-being-so-nice' present before explaining that she ended all her romantic relationships haphazardly.

I had a thousand excuses for Rachel being like that – that she was dissociative, young, ashamed. On the phone now, I listened as Mum retold the story. 'She's all about refugees and the poor,' she said bitterly, 'but it's all about *her*, Khin. She's a narcissist. That whole family sound awful.'

I changed the subject by telling Mum that I'd decided to make an appointment with a lawyer.

'Family courts don't trust men,' she said immediately. 'You *need* a lawyer. I used to take battered women to the family court in Perth, and the judges heard all these atrocious stories about the husbands. Those women *needed* protection, Khin. The fact that Rachel doesn't won't make a difference. You'll be seen like *all* men if you're in front of a judge.'

After the call, I thought about the family court and Rachel's mother. On the second day of Mary's visit, she'd showed her hand to me while Rachel was in the shower.

'Rachel is special, Khin,' she'd said. 'I didn't … I didn't give her the … the … *political* education I did just to have her end up in the middle of nowhere married to an ESL teacher.'

The sort of family Rachel was from thought of child-rearing as a project – you carefully shaped your kids to become world-changers rather than just hoping they would survive.

Thinking back, I could hear the word *political* more clearly. Mary had stumbled on it, like it wasn't comfortable. For the Devisons, politics was quasi-religious. They were middle-class and saw themselves as below the corporate elites ruling the world, which they had enough ambition and smarts to resent. They had more financial and cultural capital than my family by a mile, but someone like Mary couldn't see that. Mary had a master's degree and a well-paid professional job. Her ex-husband was a software engineer. She had two healthy kids and a good relationship with her ex-husband. They were deeply tied to a community where they belonged. They had extended family. And talking politics over the dinner table with their children was *de rigueur*. Their privileges were plentiful, but it annoyed them to consider that.

It was easier when looking at deeply disadvantaged groups like refugees or homeless people. Such groups were blameless. Everyone else was more or less blameworthy for their failings. In other words, Mary was progressive when thinking about a distant *Other* but conservative when faced with disadvantage closer to home. It was easier to give compassion to people who were so unlike yourself that you didn't worry about them marrying your daughter.

★

Later that morning, I googled family lawyers and spoke to a woman called Layla Galatas.

'That all sounds very terrible,' she said. 'We charge $350 for an initial consultation.'

When I asked if there was an appointment tomorrow, she told me that I wouldn't get anything anywhere before next week because of the Independence Day holiday.

Mum phoned again just after midday and said she'd called Mary Devison. 'I had her phone number from one of those emails on the partner visa paperwork.'

'What did you say?' I asked anxiously.

'I got their bloody machine,' she said. 'But I gave her a piece of my mind in a message.'

I felt the room spin. 'What did you say?'

'I said I had a sick and suicidal daughter at home and that this was the last thing our family needed.'

'I think it's best you don't call again,' I said.

★

The next day, I made a quick trip across the road to print off some emails. I printed the ones Rachel and I had exchanged following our meeting at the cafe. They felt like evidence. They proved I'd told her I was leaving and wouldn't contact her; importantly, they showed that she knew this but left it out of her statement. I also printed an email showing we had planned to marry and emails that documented her asking me to come to the US to salvage things before changing her mind and asking me not to. I didn't see myself as her opponent, though I knew I needed to think like one. It felt ugly, like secretly getting ready to do public battle with your best friend.

★

The following day was the Fourth of July.

I heard fireworks in a park somewhere, and pale shades of purple glowed on the back wall of my attic. Deep booms seemed to shake my bowels loose.

On Tuesday evening, I snuck down to the grocery store. The streets made me jumpy. I kept thinking that Rachel would have friends keeping tabs on me, an exceptionally paranoid thought that inspired further feelings of shame.

On my way back to the room, I was waiting at a pedestrian crossing when a car pulled up and a strident female voice from the passenger window shouted something.

'Hey!' the woman said. 'Hey!'

When the light turned green, the car revved and I could have crossed but was frozen.

'Nice arse, baby!' the voice screeched out before the vehicle took off in a doppler of twenty-something giggles.

★

As I was packing, I found a letter from Rachel that I had put in a small compartment of my suitcase in Australia and then forgotten. On the envelope was a shiny gold sticker with her name, address and university credentials embossed on it. The letter itself was in the same handwriting as her police statement. I could see for the first time that the note read like something a teenager might have written:

Dear Khindle,

I miss you. I'm so sorry that I ran away. But I needed to, and now I'm so much better. I'm ready to be the best version of myself, and to be the honest, healthy partner that you deserve. I think that time apart will help us refocus as individuals, so that when we are together again we'll be stronger than ever. I love you so much! Yesterday I went to the gym, then my dad came over for dinner. We talked about Burmese refugees then watched a stoner movie on TV. This morning I drove Dad's Burmese refugee family to the doctor again, then looked at pictures of us. You always hold me so confidently; I don't need it, but the visual proof of your devotion is reassuring. Tonight I'm going to a poetry reading at the gay pride centre with my friend Emily. That's all for now. I'll see you tonight in my dreams. Love.

Twelve

I wasn't surprised when my sister's illness began. Mum called and said Theda had broken up with her fiancé and wasn't going to complete her broadcast journalism course. The doctors said it was depression. They prescribed cognitive behavioural therapy and anti-depressants. True to my sister's type-A personality, she embraced therapy with gusto. She even went to an intensive CBT camp.

I knew very little about cognitive behavioural therapy, but my faith in it was minimal. According to my sister, it was about noticing your negative self-talk and dispelling it as irrational. How could something like that eradicate the shame she had acquired quite rationally in a city where it was constantly reinforced that part of her was undesirable? She was still caught on our father's assertions that the white part of herself – the desirable part – was defective too. When your father and the society you live in continually tell you that part of your being is inadequate and problematic, you don't need rational self-talk; you need to express anger. You need to tell the world to fuck off. It's fine to notice thought patterns and try to change them, but that's just pissing in the wind if you can't also yell at the world for rejecting you. You need to understand the rejection wasn't your fault.

Theda's symptoms included fatigue. I wasn't surprised by this either. I didn't think of mental illness as something that happened only in your brain and thoughts. So when a new doctor suggested the origins of her illness were physical rather than mental because she had physical symptoms, I was sceptical. His name was Dr Nihal, and he was carving out a name for himself as a specialist on chronic fatigue syndrome.

I didn't know it yet, but chronic fatigue syndrome would give her a monstrous status in many people's eyes that wasn't so unlike the one we'd had as mixed-race children in a backwater part of Perth. Chronic fatigue syndrome placed her uncomfortably between mental and physical illness. In the early years, we would encounter doctors who pointed out this link, but Dr Nihal was steadfastly against it.

'It's not a mental illness,' he told my mother and sister. 'Therapy will only tire her out. She needs rest and a change of diet.'

I learned a lot about chronic fatigue syndrome over the next year. Its diagnostic term is *myalgic encephalomyelitis*. The World Health Organization would estimate there were twenty-four million sufferers worldwide. It is considered incurable, and there is debate over how to treat it. According to governing medical bodies, its cause remains unknown. Despite that, some research links it to mental health and shows therapy can help. Other research argues strongly against that. Each side produces studies that disprove the other's claims. Patients are left to choose which medical professionals to believe.

Dr Nihal explained that chronic fatigue syndrome was stigmatised because of the medical establishment's ignorance. He positioned himself as being on the cutting edge, with the latest research at his disposal.

I later learned that the term *myalgic encephalomyelitis* was coined when a mysterious illness with symptoms of chronic fatigue swept through a London hospital ward in 1955. The illness had things in common with a disease that psychiatrists had once labelled *hysteria* – now called conversion disorder. The sufferers also had symptoms that sometimes occur in people with swollen spinal cords. *Myalgic encephalomyelitis*, or 'M.E.' for short, refers to spinal cord swelling.

MRI technology later revealed no spinal swelling in people with chronic fatigue syndrome symptoms, but the label stuck nonetheless. It is more official-sounding than *chronic fatigue syndrome* and avoids the stigma of confusion between normal fatigue and what people like my sister felt.

I was uneasy about Dr Nihal. His treatment was long-term bed rest, which felt counterintuitive to me. I didn't expect Theda to push through her fatigue like an athlete, but life in bed was not an answer I thought we should embrace either. More than anything, the social isolation seemed unhealthy. She was a young woman in her twenties who needed friends and stimulation.

Dr Nihal held the line. He likened my sister's body to a faulty rechargeable battery. 'Ordinary people', he said, 'recover from exertion, but an M.E. sufferer's body doesn't. If she rests for long enough, however, her body will find ways of repairing itself long term.'

Convinced that the failure of cognitive behavioural therapy proved Dr Nihal correct, my mother dismissed my doubts. She told me Dr Nihal was an expert and I had swallowed too much new-age hippie claptrap. I didn't like being associated with people who thought positive thinking could cure illness. I didn't think that. But I couldn't shake the idea that my sister's illness was based on her dissociation from buried pain and anguish. I also questioned whether anyone's mind could be separated from their body so cleanly, but I didn't know how to express that in a way that might convince anyone.

I quickly learned that it was dangerous to voice these doubts around my sister. As she embraced the M.E. diagnosis, she also began to hear blame when suggestions of mental illness came up. Mental illness was confirmation that she had 'chosen' to be sick. She heard our father in those ideas – his certainty when we were kids that if we'd been more Buddhist we wouldn't have got colds or been bullied.

★

One summer morning I brought up the possibility of therapy with Theda. Mum had a medical appointment and had asked me to look after my sister, who needed medicines and food brought to her room by that stage. She was almost completely bedridden.

I drove to their house, and Theda and I had a nice morning together.

She was having a better day than usual with her symptoms, probably buoyed by her baby brother being there and making her laugh. I had been telling her about quirks in my dating life.

She wanted lunch at midday, so I asked if she would come out into the garden around eleven. I said I would put some cushions on a recliner chair and she could return to her bedroom whenever she wanted. When she agreed, I felt triumphant because I hadn't seen her outside the house in a year or more. I remember that she gripped my arm as we walked from the back door to where I'd set up the recliner. I sat beside her, and we chatted. Her brain fog would get worse in the coming years, but it was intermittent and relatively mild back then so we could talk if the conversation was fairly light.

'I miss my health, Minty,' she said. 'But at least we're no longer barking up the wrong tree.'

'What do you mean?'

'All that therapy when my illness is a physical thing.'

'We shouldn't completely discount therapy,' I said.

She looked at me like I'd slapped her.

'I just mean with symptoms,' I said. 'It's tough to know what's mental and physical sometimes. If some of your symptoms respond to therapy, that's just a bonus, right? Therapy is good for any of us in my opinion.'

'CBT didn't do anything,' she said.

'I'm not talking about CBT,' I said. 'I mean something deeper than that. Something where you get to think about what it meant to grow up like we did.'

'M.E. is a *physical* illness, Khin,' she said angrily.

'I know that,' I said. 'I'm just saying, our minds and bodies aren't always as separate as doctors tell us. I believe in M.E. – I *do* – but what if even just a couple of your symptoms aren't only physical?'

I spoke like that partly because of my own experiences, and partly because I had seen her symptoms shift and change a bit over the years.

Even her allergies seemed responsive to her moods, let alone her fatigue and brain fog.

'Do you really think I'd put you and Mum through this because I'm selfish?' she said.

'I don't think mental illness is selfish,' I said.

'So you just think I'm crazy?'

'We're all a bit fucked up,' I said. 'There's no—'

'*Doctors*,' she interrupted. '*Doctors* say M.E. is a physical illness, Khin. It has nothing to do with my mind. You sound just like Dad.'

★

A few weeks before that conversation, I had been at my father's house having dinner. Theda's relationship with him was more troubled than mine. I maintained a superficial connection that I'd honed to avoid bickering. When I'd first returned from Melbourne, he had tried to belittle me when we caught up. He still made me anxious if I did anything in front of him. He was prone to telling me I didn't do things mindfully enough and was controlled by Western habits. But I had come back to Perth with more confidence. I played a mantra in my head when he was around now. I repeated the words *he's a crazy man* whenever he was trying to talk down to me. He was jealous of me still, and insecure – I could see that as an adult.

Then I found the knife I'd used to attempt suicide sitting in his kitchen drawer.

'Dad,' I'd said, holding it over the kitchen counter, 'why do you have this?'

I remember the look he gave me. 'You Westerners,' he said, falling back on an old trope. 'In Burma, we don't waste good things.'

I'd never cleaned the knife after my suicide attempt. I had stuck the knife in a shoebox along with some old love letters and diaries and stored it in another box in Dad's garage when I'd left Perth.

'It still has my blood on it,' I told him. 'It's the knife I attempted suicide with.'

I had lost a lot of blood. Black coagulated bits of it were caked on where the blade met the handle.

He turned to face me. He was wearing a longyi and no T-shirt. His dark brown skin reflected the harsh neon lights he had in the kitchen (another thing that he said was Burmese – not worrying about décor). There was a Buddhist book in his hand.

'You Westerners attach too much meaning to inanimate objects,' he said. 'It's hard to find a knife that can cut a tomato well. Don't worry, I cleaned it. Those stains are permanent.'

I understood why Theda was so angry at our father. For our whole lives, he'd told us anything we suffered was our own fault. It was part of a macabre performance in which he gave his own identity as a Burmese Buddhist psychologist the dignity he felt it deserved – a dignity denied him by the Western world. I understood by my twenties that it was an inferiority complex of some kind. My mother had shared some stories of how when our father was a young psychologist working for the government with drug addicts, a new manager had entered his department and fired all the Asians, saying that there were too many of them around. My father had grown up in a dusty village with parents who'd never even finished primary school. His family had been poor. His rise to a professional position in the West was unbelievable, but it was met with a sort of racism he then denied. 'Migrants have to work twice as hard as locals,' he had repeatedly told me, never saying that such a thing was *unfair*, only that it was true.

The day after Theda and I spoke in the garden about the possibility of therapy, Mum called.

'You're not a *doctor*, Khin,' she said. 'You need to stop telling her it's all in her head.'

'I don't think it's all in her head,' I said. 'And Dr Nihal is *one* doctor.'

'This is because of your damn father,' she said. 'He's caused you and your sister so much damage.'

'I'm not Dad,' I said.

'You sound just like him,' she said.

Mum then told me that she felt like walking into the ocean and ending it all. She hated Australia and had married a man who didn't work out. She said if Theda and I fell out, there was nothing left to live for.

I apologised, and I said sorry to Theda the next day. She was quick to accept it, and we didn't speak about the conversation again. There was never any chance of Theda and I falling out. Despite her insinuation that mental illness was a choice, I never thought that way. Even if her illness were entirely mental, which wasn't what I'd been implying, I wouldn't have blamed her.

★

Not long after that, Dr Nihal suggested a walking frame for my sister. It was best to stay horizontal, he said, but a frame would do for getting around the house. He also told my mother to purchase a plastic chair so Theda could sit down in the shower. But of all the things he suggested, it was the bell that I felt most uncomfortable about. He told my sister to ring it whenever she needed something. Calling out from her bedroom expended valuable energy, Dr Nihal said, so the soft tinkle of that little bell rang out roughly every half hour instead. It mostly rang because she was lonely in her room. She was following doctor's orders but also grieving a life not yet lived.

I worried about Mum's suicidal wishes. I was familiar with them from my teen years, but they'd tapered off as she got used to being a single mother. There is a saying that any mother is only ever as happy as her least happy child, and as Theda's light dimmed, Mum's suicidal thinking resurfaced. I tried to stay detached, but it was hard. I couldn't stop the feeling that I was watching my sister's illness kill our mother.

Mum vented her anger by berating Dad sometimes. They were long divorced, but he wasn't helping with my sister's care. Mum blamed his religion for his so-called detachment from his children's suffering. 'The fucking Buddha,' she would say. 'I could kill him for what he's done to this family.'

Thirteen

'I have some unfortunate news,' the lawyer said. 'Orders of protection affect non-citizens differently than Americans. So my question to you is this …' She paused to ensure I was paying attention, her acrylic nails resting on the hardwood table in front of us. 'How do you feel about being banned from the United States for life?'

We were in a business park on the outskirts of Albany. My lawyer for the next hour was Layla Galatas, an angular woman about my age, with dark eyes and a firm handshake. She had pale skin and a large, slightly hooked nose. She wore a red skirt-suit with big shoulder pads that reminded me of an earlier decade, and her haircut reminded me of something Theda had done in the '80s.

'Think about it carefully,' she said.

'Can I represent myself in court?' I asked.

She twisted her lips. 'This area of family law crosses into criminal law in some unusual ways. I wouldn't suggest representing yourself. Use legal aid if you can't afford hiring me beyond this appointment.'

'I can do that? As a non-citizen?'

She confirmed that I could.

At the start of our meeting, she had read Rachel's statement and described the petition as weak. She said it didn't describe stalking, but she warned that judges needed to be cautious in such matters and the decision could still go against me. The burden of proof was the *preponderance of the evidence*, so a fifty per cent likelihood that I was guilty would be enough to grant Rachel's wishes.

'A judge has the information a person gives them,' she said.

'It's at the trial that things tend to come out.'

'A trial?' I asked. 'I have to come back in four weeks for something. Is that it?'

'For the preliminary, yes. But if we can't get it dismissed, a trial date will be set.'

I thought about it for a moment. I knew nothing about the law.

She uncrossed her legs and crossed them again, gently rocking a pointed black shoe. 'Go as early as possible to the courthouse on Clinton Street tomorrow. Take your paperwork. They'll give you an appointment for legal aid, but as I warn all my clients, legal aid can be unpredictable. You don't get to choose.'

'I only want six months in this country,' I said. 'I don't really know how I feel about a lifetime ban after that.'

'Well, you'd be deported immediately,' she said, looking at me with the same concern she'd shown earlier.

I turned it over in my head, unsure that I could stay in my accommodation for an extra night to visit legal aid tomorrow. I'd already booked a coach out of Albany for that afternoon and had a place booked in Syracuse – Savannah had been too expensive in the end because I would need to be back in Albany in four weeks. Going south of the Mason-Dixon Line wasn't affordable if I factored in bus trips to and from here.

Layla Galatas sat back in her chair and sighed. 'You wouldn't see someone tomorrow. But they'd give you an appointment before the appearance.'

'I'd have to stay in Albany for an appointment?'

She nodded, then said something about phone appointments. I realised that legal aid wasn't much of an option for me. I no longer trusted Rachel. She could accuse me of things if I stayed in Albany. It was sad to consider, but I knew it was a possibility and that I needed to look out for myself.

'What happens at a trial?' I asked.

'You get to tell your side of the story.' She slowly nodded as she spoke.

'We can present evidence at trial. We can cross-examine.'

'Cross-examine?'

'Ask questions,' she said. 'Go over anything left out.'

'What would happen in that situation if I was representing myself?' I asked.

'You would cross-examine Rachel, and she'd cross-examine you if she were unrepresented.'

I knew Rachel had a family friend who was a lawyer, but visions of us both questioning the other in a witness box flashed into mind, and it made me laugh with despair at the absurdity.

One of my lawyer's long bony fingers tapped my papers. She gave me an unexpectedly warm smile. 'Look,' she said. 'Judge Duggan is unpredictable. But he's analytical. If we end up at trial, I'm confident you'll win. Her petition doesn't hold up. I'd try to get some of that across in the preliminary. There's even a chance he will dismiss it without setting a trial.'

I looked up at the clock. 'I'm leaving in a couple of hours,' I said. 'I have a bus up to Syracuse.'

'You know that you don't have to leave Albany, right?'

'I know that.'

She nodded to herself slowly, then said. 'No one has the right to demand another person leave an entire city. But if you're leaving anyway, which is what you're saying ...', she paused while looking at me to check it was true, and I nodded, 'it might be worth my calling Rachel. I can say you're gone and not planning to come back. She might let this go.'

'That sounds great,' I said, knowing this had been my next line of questioning anyway. 'How much would it cost?'

'I could include it in today's fee', she said, 'if we end our appointment now.'

After that, she made photocopies of my papers and I said goodbye. I headed back to the B & B with a sense of relief, picked up my things and went to the coach station.

Fourteen

In 2005, Theda had her first psychotic break.

'What do you mean psychotic?' I asked.

'I mean psychotic,' said Mum. 'I found her in her room, surrounded by her childhood dolls, and she thinks she's talking to angels.'

I arrived at the hospital after dark, where a nurse in scrubs led me through a big open-plan ward and everywhere people rushed about. There were occupied beds along one wall, separated by thin curtains hung from the ceiling. A cacophony of sneakers squeaked on laminex around us. Someone was screaming in the distance, and as the nurse led me closer, I realised it was Theda. When I saw her it was shocking. She was on a stretcher, boosted high, with its railing up, parked with its head against a concrete pillar, and she was screaming like someone was trying to murder her.

The nurse who'd led me there was already on to her next task, so I stood for a moment trying to make sense of it. Theda's face was different. It was as if she'd been possessed. She was arching her back like a spirit inside her body wanted to break out of her torso.

I took a step towards the stretcher, and she glared at me with eyes that didn't seem human. She then shrieked aggressively and I stepped back without meaning to.

Sigmund Freud labelled the part of us driving the unconscious *das Es,* which is German for the it (later rebranded by a translator as the Id), a fundamental cluster of primal urges completely beyond our control or awareness. The person called Theda was gone that day. I was facing a creature concerned only with its own survival. It made my skin tingle because it came from someone I'd known my whole life and she clearly didn't recognise me.

Mum took me to one side and briefly explained that four security guards had been needed to hold Theda down while they injected a sedative. The head physician was being consulted because nursing staff had already given her the maximum dose.

★

A few weeks later, Theda would explain these events to me from her perspective. It started with voices saying her illness was a spiritual issue, and by the time she was in the Emergency Department, she was convinced that she'd been brought in for a live organ harvest. She thought a more deserving woman needed her insides and doctors had signed off on it. On the stretcher, she was screaming because she didn't want to die.

Over the coming years, I would learn more about psychosis. I'd learn that hallucinations alter sensory perception, and delusions are often the explanations we give ourselves for those alterations. We need a story to explain our perceptions or else we don't know how to respond to the world around us, so we interpret perceptual events as a narrative in which we are the central character. We all hallucinate a bit when a vine on the path looks like a snake for an instant. And our nervous system reacts before the rational brain realises our mistake. Our storytelling mind is immediate and only quasi-conscious because it's primed to respond to threats that arise quickly. We momentarily exist in a different story when the potential of being killed by a snake has overrun our sense of where we were heading.

Aural hallucinations are similar to visual hallucinations. People hear voices because language is almost always flowing through parts of the brain we aren't paying attention to. Our linguistic brain automatically sorts that language into two broad categories: our thoughts and outside sources. Psychiatrists call this process *source monitoring* and we barely notice it. When source monitoring fails, however, we no longer know if we thought something, heard it or read it. So some of our thoughts become 'voices' because of a malfunction in our source-monitoring brain. Why this happens and what it means is up for debate.

We usually aren't paying much attention to our self-talk because lots of it is incessant. Conscious thought is what we focus on. But when we can no longer differentiate *any* thoughts from the language uttered around us in the world, thinking and hearing become indistinct, and the boundary between unconscious and conscious thought falls away. Our brain can no longer separate compulsive unconscious thoughts from what others say. It's a kind of chaos that also breaks down the distinction between self and other.

★

The hospital staff eventually subdued my sister. Mum and I sat in plastic chairs while Theda flitted in and out of awareness in the emergency department. I don't know what Mum was thinking, but I felt our family had changed. I thought this event meant that the chronic fatigue syndrome diagnosis was in question, and it gave me hope. Before that night, we'd been untouched by the kind of mental illness people talked about in terms of 'madness'. It was Theda's greatest fear to be labelled that way, and yet falling into this might be a solution. Schizophrenia sat in a different category of mental disorder – it evoked images of people locked in a padded room as they screamed at the walls – but I didn't mind if that's what my sister had. I would learn about it, and we would face it together.

The hospital stripped my sister of her rights the next day. I had to work in the morning, but in the afternoon I visited her in a locked ward at the back of the hospital, in what seemed like a basement. I was buzzed in through a heavy door and found my mother slumped over a row of chairs in the common area, near a plexiglass cubby that was obviously for dispensing medication.

'She's still not recognising anyone,' Mum said. 'The psychiatrists are talking about schizophrenia. But she can't have that.'

'Why not?' I said.

Mum gave me a stern look. 'That's a lifelong illness, Khin.'

I remembered hearing that Mum's mother had suffered a kind of bipolar disorder. Dad had brought it up a couple of times when talking about Theda. I'd not factored such family history into things much before now and I wondered why.

Mum frowned, then furrowed her brow comically. 'She's been calling me "That person who calls herself Mother". She told me to sit on the floor because no one sits higher than "The Queen"!'

'What did you do?'

Mum shrugged. 'I just nodded along then sat on a chair anyway. She probably forgot a moment later. Her thinking is all over the place. She's not making any sense and she can't hold her attention on anything for very long.'

After that, we went into my sister's room, and I got to see for myself. The room was large with a pale green curtain splitting it down the middle. There was one other patient on the other side. Theda was awake and sitting up, her back against the wall, with a small window just above her offering an optimistic view of a bench and a stream outside. We weren't in a basement as I had thought earlier. The hospital was built on a slope and the bench was situated in some semi-bushland. The window looked unbreakable.

Theda's face still wasn't hers. She looked up as Mum and I entered. The other patient murmured, so my sister jerked her eyes towards the curtain and said in a patronising tone, 'Relax, Martha!' She then looked back at me standing in the doorway and grinned. 'Oh yes,' she said. '*Neo* is here.'

Mum and I took chairs beside the bed, and Theda started talking to herself. Mum said she'd been talking nonstop all day. Her speech was unlike anything I'd ever heard before. She was doing what I'd later learn is called *clanging*. Theories about it are vague, but clanging is a form of pressured speech (think of a high-pressure hose) most often noted in grandiose psychotic manias. The need for those words to form meaning becomes less important so long as they continue to come.

Words with similar sounds start grouping, and the result isn't entirely nonsensical, but it contains a lot of rhyme and onomatopoeia as well as stream-of-consciousness content.

Theda clanged but also stumbled upon a sentence here and there that had meaning I could understand. She would stop, listen, as if waiting for more, and then scrawl something in her notebook when this happened, which made me think she recognised some things coming out of her mouth as more comprehensible than others.

Clanging is often accompanied by *hypergraphia*, which is an obsessive need to write a seemingly nonsensical flow of words and symbols. Someone had given her an exercise book and it was open on her lap. I saw the page had words and shapes on it. Some words were written over several times in handwriting that wasn't hers, though it came from her. My sister's handwriting had always been meticulous, but this was scrawled and confident in its meaning, despite potentially being unreadable. One word written several times was *God*, and there was also *karma*. In the centre of the right-hand page, she'd drawn a triangle and written a word at each point – *Burma*, *England* and *Perth*.

'The staff said I could bring things to give her,' Mum said. 'So long as they couldn't be used as weapons.'

She had explained earlier that my sister had twisted her spectacles into an infinity symbol, then thrown them in a bin somewhere. Theda was short-sighted and had worn glasses since childhood, but Mum said she seemed to be moving about the ward without any trouble. She'd been disturbing some of the other patients, and staff had ushered her back into bed by bribing her with the notebook.

I would later discover that some people experience better vision when psychotic. Scientists in the '70s tried to study it. Researchers theorised that psychosis could alter a person's corneal curvature, meaning they didn't need glasses even if they were usually visually impaired. Likewise, the bright lights of the ward weren't worrying Theda and nor were loud sounds and speech. Hyperacuity and light sensitivity were two symptoms Dr Nihal had attributed to her chronic fatigue syndrome, but they were completely gone. She obviously wasn't fatigued either, given that she'd been difficult to keep in bed earlier. Nor was she complaining about any neuropathic pain. It was as if all her physical symptoms had been transmogrified into a psychosis.

When Theda got out of bed next, Mum tensed up. Theda grabbed a few things off the bedside table and arranged them on the floor near the foot of the bed. There was an iPod Nano in the mix, and several times she stepped back to appraise the placement of the objects as if preparing a spell of some kind. Objects were precious and meaningful. This would become a hallmark of her psychotic breaks in the coming years. But after a few minutes of rearranging, she got frustrated and snatched the iPod from the floor, then marched towards the room's dividing curtain.

'Stop her!' Mum said sharply. 'She'll flush it.'

According to Mum, Theda had been flushing various things down toilets since the psychotic symptoms had started, first at home and then in hospital.

The other patient had a sheet pulled over her head. Sharing a room with someone in my sister's state wouldn't have been easy. Theda was at the door to the adjoining bathroom and she wheeled around to face me. 'No, Neo!' she cried. 'This has to go.' She had the iPod Nano gripped tightly in one hand.

'What about the others?' I said gently.

She looked at me like I had said something important. '*Which* others?'

'The ones in trouble,' I said. 'The ones not as strong yet.'

I don't know what I was thinking but my instinct was to talk like this. I had spoken to her like this once before in another life, when we were children and she led our imaginary games. A follower has more power over a leader than they let on if they understand their role. Her head tilted slightly and I came closer. I had picked up on the traces of sense lingering in her clanging speech earlier. There had been something vague and mythic, related to her illness. She'd been talking about gods and their victims – talking to people who weren't there. Some of it was related to an illness that someone called *Theda* had. Talking about 'the others' was somehow part of that story. I knew my sister's weakness: she wanted to help people. If there were others who needed the thing she was intent on destroying, she would reconsider.

She took a step towards me, then placed the iPod Nano carefully in my palm and said, '*You* know what to do with this, Neo.'

After I had watched her eat a typical meal (no allergic reactions to various foods) for the first time in years, a nurse came in and announced it was time for patients to go into the common area for their midday medications. I was worried she would refuse, so said I would join her while Mum stayed behind.

I hadn't seen Theda around strangers in years. Once upon a time, she'd had her way of handling people that was hypervigilant and uber polite and anxious. Since her M.E. diagnosis, she had avoided people altogether. Dr Nihal said social interaction was draining and not worth risking. I no longer introduced friends or lovers to my family because of that. Theda's illness was like a landmine that strangers might set off. However, that day in the locked ward I saw my sister enter an environment that even I would have found intimidating and act as if those strangers were nothing to fear.

Before we found a place to sit, a massive man in a hospital gown stood in our way. It wasn't clear if he saw us, but he was swaying on the spot and glaring into space like he meant to tear apart the air itself. I wondered if the staff had ways of stopping unhinged men in places like this. To my surprise, Theda simply grasped hold of my hand and deftly guided us around him. 'Some people aren't well here,' she whispered conspiratorially once we had sat down to wait for the scrum around the medication-dispensing window to die down.

★

Later that day, when I felt sure there was a connection between Theda and me, I asked the staff if I could take her outside. I believed I understood what my sister's chaotic myth about her illness was. She briefly dialled it down when we'd gone to get her medication but otherwise hadn't stopped talking about it. Mum thought my sister's speech made no sense, but I disagreed – I could hear Theda trying to unpick a psychological reading of her illness by projecting it *writ large* as some kind of pop-culture or Buddhism-inspired cosmology. There was a logic to what she was clanging about. It had some sort of conflict at its centre that wasn't happening inside her, but which related to the illness 'Theda' was suffering from.

I'm not sure what the staff thought, but they didn't shut the idea down. Perhaps they knew psychotic patients were often playing out psychodramas at the core of their longer-term suffering.

There was a code-locked door leading outside and I had instructions to tackle her if she tried to run off. The nurse who let us out said that staff would keep an eye on us from their office windows. I wanted to interact with Theda away from others partly so I didn't feel so self-conscious asking her to explain some things that might seem insane to others.

Once we were outside, she stopped clanging as much and made a bit more sense. She wanted to flee the hospital, but after I'd convinced her that we couldn't do that she talked about a battle between light and darkness happening in another realm. 'Theda's' physical illness was at the centre of that conflict somehow, and it wasn't clear if light needed to win or if balance just needed to be achieved.

We sat on the small bench and I watched the passing stream as she talked about gods and monsters. I was the hero in her story. I was Neo (from *The Matrix*, I assumed), though sometimes I was Angel from *Buffy the Vampire Slayer*. At one point, she talked in terms that clearly referenced the Buddhist cosmology we'd picked up from our father. Theravada Buddhists believe in infinite realms of gods, humans and daemons – all fallible in their way, with humans being the most likely to achieve liberation from the cycles of rebirth. One story in Buddhist scripture talks of the Buddha remembering a past life as the devil-like creature Mara (who paradoxically resides in one of the heavenly realms). Mara is the one who tried to tempt the Buddha with desire as he sat in meditation under the Bodhi tree just before his shift into a state of Nirvana.

Theda was throwing out references to that complex cosmology with the same conviction and flexibility with which she alluded to the TV and movies she'd consumed in her lifetime. (Anyone who tells you fiction doesn't serve the role religion once did is short-sighted.)

'We need to help,' she said.

'How do we help?' I asked.

'We should never have been born here,' she said.

'Where?'

'Here!' she said angrily, shaking her open hand at the air. 'This realm. It wasn't right for our family. We never belonged here. It was a cosmic accident.'

She then talked about *The Mother* and *The Father*. The Father had built a prison to protect himself from this accidental rebirth, but it meant no one could reach him. The Mother was caught in a cycle of self-sacrifice as atonement for having brought us here. Neo had escaped but come back. And Theda was also in trouble, being part of this family that had been born into the wrong realm.

'We should never have come,' she said, looking around. 'It was an attempt at a better rebirth but it all turned to shit.'

★

Many years later, I learned about South Korean shamans, people who fall ill with a physical disease that is remarkably similar to chronic fatigue syndrome. Sometimes the sickness looks more like conversion disorder – shaking, paralysis and seizures. Other times it produces fatigue and pain. Either way, the community interprets it as a sign of a nascent connection with the ancestors via the body. It's a matriarchal tradition and the sufferers are mostly female. A senior woman gets called in to train the younger one on how to experience the illness, guiding her to harness the power of those altered states and provide insight to her community, which believes it has lost its moral compass in modernity.

My instinct was to see Theda's psychosis as transformative in this way. I often wondered what might happen if, instead of medicalising her illness and focusing on treatments for the individual, she were given a way of understanding it as a social phenomenon – a personal vulnerability experienced by those who manifest wider and deeper troubles in their culture. In other words, if her illness were taken for a sign or omen about how the world needs to change.

★

Her physical symptoms remained absent for two weeks as her mythic delusions continued to spill out. I learned her language better – she clanged less when I was around and talked more in whole sentences. Even Mum noticed it. Theda's face was animated and her emotions flowed freely. In this state, she reminded me of brilliant actors improvising and she seemed unafraid of her anger. But her anger wasn't a blockage or denial, because sorrow and rage flowed easily around it. I told her afterwards that it had been like watching a genius, and I meant it. For me, anger had been easier to access when I'd suffered from mental illness. I thought it was likely gendered. Women were socialised to repress anger more than men.

The psychosis began to wane after about ten days, as powerful antipsychotics drew her back. Her body language shifted. Her shoulders curved inward and her movements became less self-assured. The bold personality slowed down and got replaced by the docile, rational and tired Theda I'd seen before. Her physical symptoms returned at the same pace.

She recognised me as her brother on the ninth day.

★

After the locked ward discharged her, Dr Nihal explained the psychosis as a symptom of M.E. He said it was rare but could happen. His advice was to ignore what the psychiatrists had said about bipolar with psychotic affect (or any other mental health diagnosis) and to continue with the absolute bed rest his expertise suggested was her best hope for long-term recovery.

Fifteen

New York's countryside was a patchwork of green fields, forests and hills. The coach passed small towns with big antennae and church buildings overlooking their houses. Utes that Americans call trucks sat boldly on nicely clipped front lawns and in driveways.

Watching the landscape pass by lulled me, and I started thinking about being a kid again. Family holidays before my teens had been idyllic in Western Australia. Rottnest Island and Dunsborough and Augusta all mixed together in my mind. Long white beaches on the Indian Ocean with its icy water lapping the shore. I wasn't sure where each scene came from, but Dad was part of our tiny tribe. We camped once a year, and the usual routines and rules of childhood would fall away.

In one memory, I'm on the beach with Dad and Mum. I think it's Rottnest, but I can't be sure. Theda has ventured off towards some rocks from which teenage boys are jumping into the water. I feel normal in a way that's soon going to be over. Mum and I are close, and my head is on her lap. We're settled on a blanket with Dad next to us, and he has a fishing rod. Suddenly my mother exclaims and points at Theda standing behind a boy on the distant rocks.

'Theda!'

My sister can't be more than eleven – a small brown girl among the lithe figures of teenage boys absorbed in their fun. Our mother jumps up and starts to run, calling out her name, but Theda hears nothing. It's a tall boulder, maybe fifteen feet tall. But it's separated from the coast and the water around it has to be deep. You swim out to it, and a climb gets you to its top. Dad is also calling my sister's name now.

'Don't do it!' he shouts.

A moment later, my sister drops into the ocean below. It's a free-fall that lasts a second, but the image of her tiny body is etched into my memory. Her face is split by a grin. Every ounce of her is a pinpoint of joy, expressed in her flailing limbs as much as her face. The thrill of a risk is worth everything – ten minutes of walking up the beach, two swimming out, another fifteen getting to the top of that boulder, and five more minutes waiting her turn. She'll get told off when she returns to us, and maybe she knows that. But the moment of triumph that lasts a second is worth it.

This is who I remember before her teens seemed to suck something out of her. This is the sister who still carries a scar on her forehead from the time she defended me against some older boys in the primary school playground and ran straight into a wall after pushing one to the ground.

★

After an hour of passing through countryside, the coach was almost empty. The driver had dropped lots of passengers in one of the larger towns. Now, in the back half of the bus, it was just me and a woman texting on her phone. I became aware of a loud group of men talking near the front. I could see some of their blond hairy legs sticking out into the aisle. I figured they were the young guys I'd seen board in Albany, wearing baseball caps and university jerseys.

'That billboard is a joke, man,' one said in a voice loud enough for everyone on board to hear. Americans were louder on public transport than people back home. The woman across the aisle didn't look up, but I couldn't block them out. Dudebros, Rachel had called this kind of young American: entitled, white, arrogant and full of male privilege. It seemed likely enough. But I'd never encountered one in real life. Tuning into them now, I noticed something else. It was the insecurity in their voices. I'd reached an age where I recognised that in young men back home, but the North American version was different enough that I heard it even more clearly.

'Rikki,' another one said. 'Like, *dude*, like, I mean, like, her mom is, like, married to some Wall Street banker or some shit.'

'Yeah, man. But she's, like, a nice person.'

'She's super-frickin-hot, dude,' one of the others said.

I smiled. They were almost non sequiturs – *that girl from a rich family*, but *she's nice!* and *she's hot?* Unvoiced questions jostled just under the surface of their banter: Did women want rich men? Did attractiveness make pretty women unkind?

Masculinity wasn't a choice – it was a set of expectations you tried to navigate. I think Rachel was too young to see this. I had tried to discuss the burdens of masculinity with her, and she'd dismissed anything that wasn't strictly critical. Young women got so much unwanted attention and abuse from seemingly overconfident guys; it made sense that analysing their machismo felt like feeding the beast. I'd been victimised by the beast too, but there wasn't a daily need for defence anymore. Now, I was interested in what made men behave in certain ways. I could intuit a lot because I was also a heterosexual man, albeit quite different from the boys I'd grown up with.

As I grew older, men who would have once harassed me sometimes approached me and disclosed certain secrets. It wasn't surprising to me that they did this. Just as Benjamin and Liam and Quin had, these guys saw something non-threatening about me that they were occasionally drawn to. One or two even made passes at me, convinced I must be gay, only to discover I wasn't interested.

By the time I was in my thirties, I had concluded that stoic masculine types are often full of anxiety. It's anxiety that gets expressed in sexual desire or aggression, but it's more interesting than that. If you aren't upsetting or attracting them, you can perceive many boys and men thinking about expectations they aren't sure they can meet. Their anxiety is often focused on women. Macho guys belittle feminine things and look down on women, but they are also scared, desperate to embody what's 'masculine' so they can be attractive. It's about love – they want to be loved. And they also want each other's love in its only acceptable form: respect. Getting a 'hot' girl is so often about the status she confers on you among other men. *He must be valuable if he can get her!* Maybe that's all about wanting dominance. But it's hard not to see it as a craving for acceptance. Alain de Botton called status a generalised love that we crave from our peers.

As I listened to the boys at the front of the coach, I thought of being young. So much of it was experimenting. It was trial and error against a backdrop of media, movies and gossip about what you were supposed to be like according to whether you had a penis or a vagina. The Buddhists had been right when they said gender was synonymous with suffering. I put in headphones and tuned out, glancing out the window in time to see a slender red silo in the distance, topped with a white cap like an armless toy soldier.

★

When the coach pulled into Syracuse a couple of hours later, the dudebros stayed onboard and I got off. I crossed the car park to meet a middle-aged man in slacks and a dark long-sleeved shirt, waiting by a black SUV. He introduced himself as Michael and shook my hand. We'd already spoken on the phone and he was pleased to see me. He had dark, wavy hair and chalky skin with the well-manicured beard of a man who cared what people thought about his grooming.

'Mosta 'Cuse is struggling right now,' he said as we pulled out of the station. He pointed to a demolished corner lot with cracked concrete foundation blocks. 'See that?' he said. 'Pull it down, build it up – keeps people busy, I guess. People get into trouble when they aren't. Round and round for no good, though. The GFC hit us hard here.'

I smiled and said something agreeable.

I'd not heard of Airbnb until a few days earlier, when I'd discovered it up in my attic, looking for a place to go. It was still new, even in the States. I had paid Michael a monthly rate that wouldn't bankrupt me.

I'd also had a financial windfall when the manager of the Albany B & B refunded my rent for the days I would no longer be staying. She'd been quite understanding, perhaps taking pity when I explained everything about the police. She'd even told me I was welcome to stay again if I needed to be back in Albany for court.

As we drove into downtown Syracuse, I recognised an industrial city. It was cluttered with buildings that looked more functional than stately. The pedestrians weren't as smartly dressed as those in Albany. A concrete tangle of overpasses went by, and I noticed a billboard advertising a gun shop. I wished for a moment that I had a camera with me and realised I was falling back into the mindset of a stranger in a strange land who'd come to see what it was like.

'IBM would have regretted that,' Michael said. 'They wanted to fill the void, you see? It didn't take – I mean, it's not enough for people to have opportunities, they need *training*.'

'Makes sense,' I said.

'You have to retrain people,' he reiterated. 'It's all good that we have to change, but a lot of people are supporting families. They don't have the option to stop working. People need the healthcare that's tied to their jobs. I've heard that in some countries it's single-payer. Government pays all. That would be different. What's healthcare like in Australia?'

'It's free.'

He thought for a second. 'We won't get that here. We have Medicaid, but people fall through the gaps. Obamacare is meant to help with that. A lotta people don't like the idea of it, though.'

I thought how strange the phrase 'single-payer' was. What did it show about a culture that something I considered a human right was casually defined by who paid for it? How did things like that affect a person's outlook? Rachel had told me about her country's ruthless realities, but could I really understand their significance without living here? Maybe this was another aspect of her culture I'd failed to properly consider. Her assertions about my earning power when ending our relationship had caught me off guard. She didn't come from poverty, but she lived in a world where these pressures are deeply ingrained.

★

After we reached downtown, we circled the business district's main square and Michael pointed to a franchise cafe. He said it would be a good place to write. I'd explained 'writing' as my purpose in coming to Syracuse, since with Airbnb you needed to give a reason.

'I'm sure it will work out,' he said brightly.

I logged his enthusiasm and nodded. People I knew back home wouldn't have been so encouraging. Rachel said tall poppy syndrome was an alien concept in America. How strange that in a country where healthcare is denied as a human right, blind optimism would be the norm.

As we left the business district, the view outside abruptly changed. The first thing I saw was a three-storey wooden colonial mansion leaning to one side, with all its windows smashed out. The sidewalk was broken, and rusty cars lined the curb. It took a moment to realise that all the pedestrians were black. Further down the street, other derelict buildings buckled in disrepair. They were old wooden mansions subdivided into poor people's apartments.

'It's not so safe around here,' Michael said. 'Don't worry. I live on the other side.'

A mess of junk and plastic toys littered one of the sandy verges. I had the obvious thought that grass was a luxury. On a few corners, young black guys in loose gear were hanging about in groups and looked like they were advertising something dangerous.

'You're hiring a car, right?' Michael said.

'Can I get to the city without going through here?' I asked.

'Catch cabs,' he said.

I felt my stomach clench a bit at the idea that I needed something I couldn't afford.

We pulled up at a set of traffic lights and an elderly woman, curled over a thin metal walking frame, glared at our conspicuously shiny SUV. As we pulled away, I felt both relief and shame, but Michael just kept nattering on about something to do with Syracuse's history, and I wondered if living in the States meant you became numb to neighbourhoods like this. It seemed much too poor for a rich country, and it was shocking because of that. Rachel had talked about America's inner-city poverty but I'd not actually seen it until now, nor did movies communicate its visceral reality. She'd explained its racial origins. The mass production of cars in the 1950s turned them into a typical middle-class commodity and allowed white families to move to the suburbs. Poor black families were left to ring the city centres. It was the opposite of Perth's urban landscape, where poorer suburbs generally appeared the further you got from the centre. I'd not even considered rough inner-city areas when booking my accommodation.

'We're around here,' Michael said brightly.

We turned a corner, and as quickly as the ghetto had appeared it vanished again. We were on a well-kept street with lawns and the *tat-tat-tat* of reticulated sprinklers watering front yards on a bright summer day.

The SUV stopped beside a colonial mansion with two crisp flags hanging from angled poles below its upper windows.

★

A couple of hours later, I was sitting on the bed of my new room, answering questions online about my height, age, ethnicity and income. The bedroom was tiny compared to the one in Albany. It barely contained the bed, and it had three doors – one to the hall and two to other people's bedrooms. (Michael had assured me those wouldn't be opened.) There also seemed to be an indefinite number of people living in the house. I'd met Michael's sister downstairs upon arriving, and one of my bedroom's adjoining doors led to his elderly mother's room. I heard her cough every now and then.

I felt trapped. I was also worrying about the ghetto separating me from the city centre. Usually, in a new location, I would go outside and get to know my surroundings, but instead I'd started looking up bus connections. The local transport website had confused me, so I'd begun putting my details into an internet dating website for some inexplicable reason.

Part of me knew that Rachel's dating already was her way of handling the emotions of our breakup. At the same time, Rachel had talked about being bold. I wanted something new in my life – a different world of some kind. If I had it my way, I wouldn't ever return to the life I'd left in Australia. Immediately dating again seemed especially 'American' to me. If this experience had taught me anything, it was that my typical way of handling things wasn't working.

I also needed friends. Sex and intimacy weren't on my mind, but having a little bit of human interaction was important, and dating could provide that. I might find some friends too.

The first question was about my wage. I dealt with this by choosing a respectable figure that would have been numerically true if I'd been working full-time back home and Australian dollars were equal to American ones. It felt a bit like lying, but I figured that the American ethos involved bending the truth sometimes. I also wrote that my job was 'working with refugees', which was technically true, though I wondered why I wouldn't say that back home. It would be an attractive trait to many women there, but I never explained my job that way to people at parties. In my own culture, I downplayed the things I was genuinely proud of.

The next page wanted my height and ethnicity. I wasn't happy with my race options. The drop-down menu offered *black, white, Asian* or *Hispanic*. I selected *Asian*, but it made me uncomfortable so I changed it to *white*. Then I felt guilty and changed it back, partly because I realised people would see my photo. I changed it back to white once more before moving on. People could make up their own minds from the photos.

After I was done, I browsed to see who I might message and realised that no one in Syracuse was using this website.

That night I woke up several times with a mix of dread and nightmares banging around my head. I dreamed I was back in Australia and couldn't remember how I had got there. I felt panicky about Theda and Mum. Then I heard Michael snoring on the other side of his door and my sense of place awkwardly adjusted. I was in America. I was safe. Despite the disorientation, relief washed over me like a cool breeze on a hot day.

<h1 style="text-align:center">Sixteen</h1>

After her psychosis, Theda and Mum seemed less sure about Dr Nihal. Mum began to remember times when Theda had acted strangely in the past – times when she might have had a mild psychosis.

Although leadership had never been my role in the family, I sensed a moment of responsibility as the only person who still talked to everyone regularly.

'You want me to look after her?' Dad said when I called him.

'I can't do it,' I said. 'Mum is wavering and we have an opportunity to push back against the M.E. diagnosis.'

'They only listen to people who agree with them,' he said bitterly.

I swallowed my annoyance and told him that if he was willing to help, things might be different now.

It felt strange talking to my father like a conspirator. Theda still spoke about him with angst and despair, and I was disappointed that he'd not found a way of remaining on better terms with her. But although he was difficult and would rave on about Buddhism, he had the same ideas I did about the M.E. treatments. He wouldn't be answering her bell every half hour. Maybe it would prove to be a mistake, but I figured we were reaching a point of desperation. For a proper go, however, Mum would need to be out of Theda's reach.

I called Mum and told her I wanted to give her some money to take a trip. It wasn't much, but it would cover fuel. I said, 'You've always wanted to cross the Nullarbor.'

She was nervous, but she considered what I had to say.

A week later, she drove over the Darling Escarpment and started her journey into Australia's empty interior. It was in a little camper van she'd bought a few years earlier. She still hated Australia, but she'd grown to accept it as her fate and had been talking about travelling across it when Theda got better. That talk had been around for a few years, but she was finally doing it. Her plan was to be away for three months.

Theda called me after two days and told me our father was killing her. She said, 'He doesn't believe in M.E.'

'Give it time,' I cooed.

'He blames me,' she wept. Then she told me that a year ago she'd talked to him about feeling suicidal, and he'd said that if suicide was her karma then so be it.

'I fucking hate him,' she said.

★

The next day I drove over and spoke to them both. I knew his calling her suicidality karma was typical. It was a side of him that had made me worry about this caring arrangement. He'd said things like that to me in the past. Mum couldn't understand why I still spoke to him, but I saw him more clearly every year. He was a man who denied an inferiority complex he was nursing. Because he couldn't see it about himself, almost everything he did was an unconscious response to it. Whenever he put Theda or me down, it was like he was trying to prove himself to himself.

'Don't try to change things too quickly,' I said to him.

'You think your sister has the physical illness?' he asked angrily.

I looked at him for a moment. I'd told him so many times about my doubts. He simply didn't listen. I think I also understood something I would repeatedly see over the following years: polarisation means people can't hear each other. Mum was convinced that Theda's sickness was physical, and Dad believed it was mental. A pragmatic approach would have seen them cooperate somehow despite that difference, but Dad couldn't let go and Mum held just as tightly to Dr Nihal's assertions.

Years later, I would read an article in *The British Medical Journal* suggesting to doctors that they lie to their patients about treatments for M.E. Certain psychological treatments had proven helpful but were controversial among patients who followed the advice of other doctors mired in opposing research, so the journal suggested GPs refer patients to cognitive behavioural therapy without telling them it was psychotherapy. It was another example of the seemingly intractable tension when people disagree about the cause of a problem. Research I would discover later highlighted that an illness needn't be psychological in origin for psychological treatment to be helpful. If something helps, that's enough.

★

The next day I was over again and Dad explained his routine. He wasn't making her lunches but he'd bought easy-to-prepare lunch food. He gave her dinner in bed but encouraged her to walk to the letterbox once a day to retrieve the mail. That seemed perhaps the right balance to me, but Theda's anger was potent. She was animated and actually seemed a bit better for it, though that wasn't how she saw things.

'Dad will make me *sicker* in the long run,' she said.

'We should just try this way,' I said gently. 'After the psychosis—'

'Dr Nihal has *explained* the psychosis,' she snapped. 'Psychiatrists don't know *M.E.* Dr Nihal is one of the only doctors in Australia who understands it. Can't you see that, Khin?'

★

I visited every day after that. Mum called halfway through the following week and said Theda had been telling her what our father was doing.

'You have to convince your father that M.E. is real,' she said.

'I thought the point was to try his way of caring for her?'

'The point was to give me a break,' she said.

Confused and worried, I hung up the phone and said nothing more to Dad or Theda.

Mum called again the next day. I expected her to be upset with me, but her voice was excited. 'I parked at a trucker bed-down here on the highway,' she said. 'I wanted to walk out into the desert.'

I could picture her amid an endless barren landscape. Trucker bed-downs are places where the shoulder of the road is wide so that long-haul truckers can park and sleep. They aren't near other human activity, like petrol stations or roadside stores, so no one would notice an abandoned vehicle if she got lost on foot.

'You've always liked deserts,' I said.

'They're so silent, Khin,' she said wistfully.

She told me how she'd walked out onto the Nullarbor plain. She'd done it without water or a compass, which was obviously dangerous, not to mention that underneath its flat surface the landscape was honey-combed with caves that could collapse. She'd trekked for about an hour in what she thought was a straight line and had turned back thinking she'd find the road but had not found it. She'd eventually climbed a lit-tle desert tree as the sky was getting dark, looked for signs of life and spotted the tiny red shape of a moving car in the distance. She'd then lined up some bushes and walked until she hit the road, miles from where she'd left it.

'My van wasn't anywhere,' she said. 'So I hitched until I found it again. We went about ten kilometres in one direction, couldn't find it and then went in the other.'

'Be careful out there,' I said.

★

The following day, she called and said she was returning to Perth. 'Your father has let us down,' she said. 'He's going to set back Theda's recovery by years if I don't come home.'

I pleaded for her to let things run their course but she'd made up her mind. She'd been in contact with Theda and Dr Nihal earlier that day and both agreed she needed to come back.

She must have driven almost continuously, because she pulled up at my father's house in her dust-covered van three days later. It was years since we'd lived in the divided house. Now Dad was north of the river and Mum lived south. We hauled my sister's belongings back to Mum's place, and Mum stopped me in the driveway. 'Khin,' she said. 'I love you. But if you keep talking about mental illness, you won't be able to visit Theda anymore. It's too damaging. If you and your father keep blaming her, it *will* damage her mental health.'

'I'm not blaming anyone,' I said.

'What do you think she hears when you say this is all in her head? How can anyone *make* their body sick with their mind? I accept that you had a mental illness. Hers is different.'

I didn't have expertise to argue back with, just instinct. I tried to explain that I thought mental illness was in the body too, and that on top of that I believed repressed emotional pain could resurface as physical symptoms. I tried to explain why I thought this by relating it to my own experiences. But she just looked at me with disappointment. 'No one would fake this, Khin,' she said.

★

If there was a lesson for me in the second half of my twenties, it was about control and loss. To see a death happening slowly – and someone whom I loved dragging down my mother, who now also talked regularly about wanting to die – was painful in a complex way. It hurt because I thought I knew a solution that they wouldn't consider. Whether I was right or not didn't change the fact that I constantly felt I should be speaking up more. I felt I was betraying them not to push against their certainty and Dr Nihal's diagnosis. But it also felt like a betrayal to *keep* pushing, and it would certainly damage my relationship with them if I did. So I bit my tongue, and it was how I imagine it might be to love a drug addict. I was witnessing my loved ones slowly dying, and the one thing I thought might help was a solution they rejected.

A few weeks later, Theda wrote Dad a letter asking him to talk and he ignored it.

'I need him to say he doesn't blame me for my illness,' she told me. 'I'm different from you. You just ignore him. I *can't*, Khin. It hurts too much.'

He never wrote back and she vowed never to speak to him again.

I repaired my relationship with Theda. I apologised definitively and said I wholly believed in the M.E. diagnosis and treatment. It wasn't a total lie, because I did believe in the diagnosis – an illness needed a label. But I didn't accept that it had no links to trauma and mental illness, at least not in my sister's case.

After a few months, Theda wrote Dad another letter saying she would no longer think of him as her father. My mother and Theda now lived in a world almost entirely cut off from anyone except the doctors I thought were damaging us.

★

As the months passed, Mum suspected I still had doubts about Theda's diagnosis, so she regularly sent me documents on M.E. that affirmed her side of the debate. One of the documents was called *The Canadian Guidelines for ME/CFS* and described M.E. as a wholly biological disease with no mental health links in either cause or treatment options. I couldn't understand all its technical language, but I could tell the research it cited wasn't conclusive. I also knew that big medical bodies like the Centers for Disease Control said the cause was unknown. They also noted that a clinician's diagnosis was the only available test for M.E.

As I became more scientifically literate in later years, I would come to see a denial of uncertainty in that Canadian document. For me, the most disturbing assertion was this:

ME (Chronic Fatigue Syndrome), classified as a neurological disease in the WHO ICD, cannot also be classified as conversion disorder, which is classified as a mental or behaviour disorder.

It was in a bold typeface and was clearly meant to be the most important claim on that page. But I didn't understand how it could be applied to such a poorly understood illness. How we classify something doesn't change what it is. If M.E. and conversion disorder share symptoms, and neither can be tested definitively, what does such a claim really prove?

Fatigue and pain are among the most common symptoms that cause debate over mind versus body. Distinguishing mental disorders from bodily ones isn't always straightforward. Conversion disorder is what the ancient Greeks called *hysteria* and treated with orgasms. It is shrouded in historical absurdities like that, but its roots go as far back as ancient Egyptian medical texts. It has been rebranded over and over through the centuries, and the famous psychiatrist Pierre Janet was the first to give something approaching the modern theory of its aetiology. He saw it as an illness caused by repressed emotional distress about experiences a person couldn't process linguistically.

In the past, doctors have misdiagnosed multiple sclerosis, endometriosis and motor neuron disease as forms of conversion disorder. Misdiagnosing a physical illness as conversion is dangerous because doing so stops research and leads patients towards the wrong treatments.

Nonetheless, proven physical symptoms of conversion disorder include paralysis, blindness, unconsciousness, seizures and digestive disruption. And to misdiagnose conversion disorder as a physical illness is dangerous too because it also pushes patients towards treatments that will never cure them.

There is a third option. Horrendous physical outcomes don't always fit the mind–body binary. Takotsubo cardiomyopathy is a heart condition that can kill you, but it is most often caused by grief. It is diagnosed on an echocardiogram and attempts to cure it include both psychological and physical treatments.

Illnesses that confound the mind–body binary feel counterintuitive because we've been socialised to believe disease is more clear-cut. But medical science doesn't support a clear division in many cases.

For example, post-traumatic stress disorder damages the hippocampus in ways that can be seen in brain scans. Women who've suffered intimate partner violence often have altered neurological and gastrointestinal systems. Crohn's disease and endometriosis link to psychological trauma also. None of these conditions fit nicely into a mind–body binary.

In 2015 the world's most prestigious award for health writing, the Wellcome Book Prize, was awarded to a senior London neurologist, Suzanne O'Sullivan, who recognised that culture was lagging behind the science. In one chapter of her book, *It's All in Your Head*, she argues that M.E. is likely a form of conversion disorder, which I'm not sure I agree with. But whether or not she is correct, her conclusion about the mind–body relationship in some illnesses could hardly be more sensible: she says that society is the responsible party, not the patient:

> There is an unofficial ranking system for illness in which psychiatric disorders are the out-and-out losers. Psychiatric disorders manifesting as physical disease are at the very bottom of that pile. They are the charlatans of illness. We laugh at them.

The basic mechanism by which the body demonstrates mental distress is present when we blush, cry or shake. High blood pressure is another well-understood physical symptom that psychological disturbances can cause. We accept all these things until a more chronic problem appears. Then the stigma raises its head. We believe that overwork and job stress can damage our bodies, but when job stress is replaced with trauma, and the damage to our bodies seems ongoing, resistance to the idea gets stronger. We become sceptical.

During the years of Theda's suffering, a debate was going on far above my family's heads. Simon Wessely, an M.E. researcher at Oxford University, became the focus of controversy and media attention in the early 2000s. Advocacy groups were trying to shut him down because he wrote that multiple studies had shown mental health treatments were effective in treating M.E. People started sending him bomb threats and turning up at his lectures with knives.

Later that decade, the head of Imperial College's infectious diseases department – a woman called Myra McClure – got drawn into the conflict around M.E. when she discredited a study linking it to a well-known virus called XMRV. Parts of the M.E. advocacy community began stalking and publicly attacking her. She got death threats and eventually quit studying chronic fatigue syndrome, stating that she was exhausted by the harassment.

On the other side of the equation were researchers like Malcolm Hooper. A Sunderland University medicinal chemistry professor, Hooper was so convinced that M.E. has no mental health links that he campaigned to quash a report from the Office of the Chief Medical Officer in the UK. In the report were several passages on the possible effectiveness of mental health treatments for M.E. patients. Hooper broke professional protocol and campaigned publicly for the report's retraction before it was published. Six scientists who'd been involved in writing that report quit in anger.

Research supported both sides of the debate. Some researchers pointed to biological differences in M.E. patients, arguing that this was proof of the disease's physical cause. Others pointed to the apparent success of psychological treatments, arguing that this proved it had a mental origin.

Later, I would develop a theory about why this happened. I would get the idea after reading about a study on Parkinson's disease where some patients were given a placebo. The placebo seemed to help their shaking despite the fact that no one believes Parkinson's disease has a psychological origin. When I told a friend about this study, she became very uncomfortable and said that it wasn't fair to imply that something as devastating as Parkinson's disease could be in the mind. But the study didn't prove that Parkinson's disease was in the mind. Nor did it offer to cure it using psychotherapy. It simply showed that some Parkinson's symptoms could be affected by our unconscious mind.

Seeing my friend react so negatively helped me understand why people with M.E. resist mental health treatments so fiercely. Part of it is what Suzanne O'Sullivan says about diseases existing in a hierarchy, with some accorded more dignity than others. But most is about wanting to avoid being labelled a monster. That is something anyone would want to avoid.

★

Theda's psychotic breaks became a regular occurrence in our lives after Mum's trip across the country's interior. I came to think of them as 'visitors' who arrived about once every nine months and occupied my sister for a couple of weeks each time. They weren't totally unwelcome, because they vanquished her physical symptoms for the duration of their stay.

She'd be forced into a locked ward and pumped full of antipsychotic medicines. Psychiatrists would try to diagnose her with something akin to conversion disorder and with one of the mood conditions that could include psychosis. She'd get released, and Dr Nihal would blame the M.E. and tell us to ignore the psychiatrists.

I was Neo or Angel during most of these psychotic breaks. She *clanged* and delved into the same metaphors about our family and place. During her second break with reality, she talked about a past life in ancient Egypt, where she'd lived among some priests who'd deemed her a kind of half-caste, which meant she'd never been assured of her role in the church but could reside on its grounds. She told me that she'd once crossed into a part of the temple that was off limits for impure people, and her punishment had been gang rape before being buried alive. That trauma was why Theda was sick, she said. It needed to be rectified, drawn into the light and the wrongdoers held to account.

★

I got to know the workings of Perth's locked wards in the coming years. Psychotic patients aren't easy to manage, and Theda was often at the top of the list. She pranced around naked sometimes. Nurses at one ward got frustrated with her and locked her in a room for hours. When they refused to answer her pleas for a toilet break, she pissed on the floor. After they let her out, she dumped a jug of water over another patient's head because she hallucinated that he was on fire. I saw her that afternoon, and she wasn't traumatised by the events of the day whatsoever. She simply had hatred towards the nurses, but their bullying was *their* problem, not hers. It led me to wonder if perhaps some trauma that becomes illness rests on the repression of anger at those who've hurt you. It was atypical of Theda to blame others for their abuse. Usually, her first port of call was to blame herself. But when she was psychotic, she externalised and aimed that blame at others without a second thought, and it was healthier. Psychotic Theda was righteous. Her anger flashed at people who deserved it and some who didn't, but it never turned inwards and damaged her. Perhaps that partly explains why her physical symptoms vanished when she was like that. Everything about her spilled out instead of turning sour inside.

When I saw her like this, it gave me hope. It once made me think about a time she had come to a Buddhist talk with me. This was before her illness struck. She came to the Buddhist centre in Nollamara with me but wanted to sit apart. I didn't understand why until question time. She asked the monk if karma was just an excuse to blame victims for their suffering. I remember feeling proud of her for having the nerve to ask that in a hall full of Asian-born devotees. It took courage but was typical of the role we played between Asian and non-Asian. On the way home from the centre, she asked if I was mad at her for becoming a spectacle.

'Why would I be?' I said. 'You had no choice but to ask that.'

She paused for a moment then said, 'I want to help people who've not been given a voice.'

I was living in Melbourne at the time and visiting Perth at Christmas. Even then, I remember thinking that *she* had a story too. She just didn't think of herself as someone who deserved to speak it. And in later years, when that voice came out as psychotic delusions mimicking the tensions of our youth, it was not much different from how I imagine fiction writers express themselves. The core of her story was there, fighting to be heard in a melodramatic form that captured its essence. And that's when her physical symptoms disappeared each time – when her story came out.

Part Three

Seventeen

I chose to walk through the ghetto because I needed a way into town. I'd woken up in Michael's house, wanting a plan for the day. I was also curious.

I would later discover that Syracuse had the highest concentration of black poverty in America that year, which isn't so surprising given its industrial past and the transitions in the US that decade. I'm glad I saw it, even if it wasn't the wisest thing to do at the time.

I remember young guys wearing baggy jeans, hogging the sidewalk as they sauntered with their boxer waistbands showing. Some wore jeans so low that I couldn't fathom how they kept them from dropping below the knee altogether. Black inner-city masculinity in Syracuse had its own body language. It was flamboyant but full of heft. It was different to Perth machismo, which is predominantly Anglo-Saxon and stiff. It made me think of throwing down cash on a card table. It also made me think of guns, because it was the body language of LA gangster movies I'd seen.

I passed a group of five guys slung around the entrance to a corner store, and I felt their eyes follow me. I wondered how conspicuous I was in a suburb populated entirely by people of African descent. I decided to get off the main drag to draw less attention, then realised it is best to be among the crowd when you're worried you might be targeted for something. I was struck once again by the obviousness of poverty and despair. The buildings were falling apart and no one looked happy.

I passed a group of young men arranged so that anyone walking towards them would be inclined to step into the gutter, but I forced myself to avoid eye contact and walk straight ahead until they parted just enough to let me through. I was close enough to smell aftershave.

When I turned another corner and found an even quieter street, I saw a girl. She was the only person around, playing with a rusty pram outside a derelict house. She was tiny, with dark brown eyes and braided hair. She stared at me with unabashed curiosity that in my anxious state I interpreted as an accusation. A pile of rusting paint cans was near a deck, and I assumed she belonged to the house. I couldn't help but want to get away from her. Everything seemed to point out that I was lucky and she was not.

When I was more lost than a feather in a gust of wind, I finally decided to ask for help.

'Sup?' a man in his sixties said as I approached.

He was standing with another man outside a community centre of some kind. The older one was overweight and cherubic, and the other was darker and about twenty, wearing a button-down shirt.

'Sorry,' I said. 'I'm lost.'

'You what?'

'I'm lost. I was hoping to get downtown?'

The cherub-man pointed a chocolate-brown finger down the road in the direction I was already walking and said something I didn't catch. He immediately went back to speaking to the other man and I had no choice but to ask if he could repeat it. He stopped talking and turned to face me with an air of dismay. After a moment of looking at me, his head tilted slightly. 'Where you from?' he asked.

'I'm not sure,' I said. 'Maybe back that way a bit.' I looked in the direction I'd walked from and waved a hand.

He frowned, then chuckled. 'I mean, what country? You, like, from England or some shit?'

Realising I was a novelty, I said that I was Australian, and a smile appeared on his face. He lifted one eyebrow comically, and his other eye got smaller as if peering into a crevice. He glanced briefly at the younger man, then said, 'You mean *Australia* as in the other side of the damn world?'

'That's right,' I said.

The young man smiled slightly. The cherub-man tilted his head more and aimed his peering eye closer. 'You mean kangaroos and shit?'

I nodded and told him yes. Then he asked if I had ever seen a kangaroo and I said they had bounced around in some of the northern suburbs of my city. He was delighted by this.

'You say you living round here?' he said when he'd finished quizzing me about the kangaroos.

'Not far,' I said, pointing up the road again.

He giggled to himself, then turned back to the young guy. 'I mean, we *done* mind the tourists. We don't get'ny round here, though. Do we?'

The younger man was nodding and grinning broadly now. The older one seemed to topple forward a bit, chortling with delight, and he gave me the directions again, much more slowly, checking that I understood.

As I left, I heard them laughing.

★

Before leaving the area, I encountered one other person up close. It was in an underpass I needed to walk through. It was dark and precisely the kind of place where you got yourself mugged. Halfway through, a tall figure rose and came lurching towards me. My heart skipped a beat, but the next moment I realised it was a woman out of her mind. As she passed into a beam of dull sunlight, I saw that she was elderly. She looked fit, and had grey hair shaved to her scalp, but her eyes were vacant and unfocused. Long limbs flailed at the empty space between us and she mumbled something, then lurched past. It wasn't until she was almost gone again that I saw her holding a charred glass pipe in one hand.

★

In the evening, I phoned Mum. I described the ghetto and the addict under the bridge. I was glad to have something other than personal worries to talk about, and Mum seemed relieved and curious. We had always shared a deep empathy for people who were down and out.

'Life is luck, Khin,' she said, repeating a phrase I had associated with her for much of my adult life. 'We could have ended up like that if we'd been born into the same circumstances.'

I went to sleep that night thinking about my mother. She talked about luck as the key factor in life. She didn't blame people for their messed-up lives. She was no Mary Devison: she couldn't have discussed politics to save her life. But she had natural compassion. She wasn't trained in abstract thinking, but she had given Theda and me our emotional outlooks on the world.

Eighteen

After our father's failed attempt at caring for Theda, Mum continued down the treatment paths Dr Nihal suggested. He sent my sister to specialists in sequence. We occasionally stumbled across one who said Theda's illness was related to mental health, but Dr Nihal mostly helped us avoid that. And when we encountered one who said such things, Dr Nihal noted it for his own future reference, and we abandoned that specialist once their stance on the matter was clear.

I began to see the search for treatments as an endless cycle. There was a network of doctors willing to engage uncertainty with a purely physical lens. Any new treatment from these doctors and practitioners would lift Theda's spirits for a while, and her symptoms would retreat in synchrony. Then her symptoms would return and she'd tumble into despair. It happened like that every time, and it was like watching someone go through a string of failed marriages, replete with dependents and mixed finances. In other words, it was traumatic, and it slowly chipped away at her faith. Theda wasn't just looking for help, she was looking for a reason not to kill herself.

Mum's superannuation vanished on these treatments. She didn't have much to start with because she'd been a housewife until her late forties and dental nursing didn't pay well. But a legal loophole let her use what little there was on family health needs not covered by Medicare. She'd already paid off the little duplex she and Theda lived in, thanks to a car accident during a trip to see a patient when she was a dental nurse. She'd got a worker's compensation payout; her hands could no longer do the job she was trained for, but it paid her mortgage. I don't know what would have happened if that wasn't the case.

Now she was living off Centrelink's carer allowance. Theda's treatments ate up the disability payment she was on. It was hand to mouth.

There is a business model for medical uncertainty. Some Western doctors are part of it, but also many alternative practitioners. These practitioners know how many patients have tried and failed with Western medicine. Many vocally oppose Western medicine in their advertising-speak but not in their ruthless billing practices.

During those years, two large bookcases appeared in Mum's house. One was in the kitchen and the other in the laundry. They housed treatments that ranged from tinctures to homeopathic remedies, and flower essences to opiates, benzos and nutritional supplements. Mum and I used to joke that she was part home owner, part pharmacy.

On one of the upper shelves were a few books by Western doctors who specialised in M.E. Their titles gestured at the controversial nature of the diagnosis and flagged the idea that mainstream doctors were ignoring suffering. I could have learned the term 'invisible illness' from these titles alone, but Theda taught it to me also. The term refers to an illness without symptoms that are visible to the untrained eye. A suffering person might as well not exist without a diagnosis if their symptoms are invisible. They aren't functioning in society, nor are they accepted as people deserving of compassion.

Thinking about diagnoses, I sometimes wondered what defines intangible things. It's hard to make people believe in what they can't see. Believing is even harder when you can't perceive the reason for something's existence. Sickness is like that. People need an explanation before they'll accept that someone will need to draw on society's collective resources because of an illness. A sick person costs society, family and friends. Diagnosis explains why that's okay.

This is how I learned to understand the difference between disease and illness. A disease makes us sick, whereas an illness is how we experience that disease. When our disease is treated as suspicious, our illness includes shame. People want a diagnosis so that their illness doesn't make living with their disease worse than it has to be.

Diseases like M.E. have a complicating factor called a heterogeneous patient group. One label covers individuals who might be suffering from different diseases. Having a label helps sufferers face illness together and with less shame. But it potentially muddles up people with different conditions. That might get in the way of them finding the treatments that could work best for them.

★

In 2008, Dad told us he was leaving Perth. More accurately, he told me. I then relayed it to my mother and sister. As a retiree, he wanted to pursue his dream of working with refugees on the Thai–Burma border. It let him apply both his love of psychology and his love of Buddhism while simultaneously being admired by well-heeled Western aid workers whose quasi-religious mission was to help the world's poor brown people. They would give him some of the respect he'd never had in Australia.

'You could still repair the relationship with Theda,' I said. 'If you stay it will help.'

'I can't put my life on hold, son,' he said.

'Why not just accept her diagnosis even if you don't agree? What difference does it make at this stage?'

'I won't go against what I believe,' he said. 'Not for anyone.'

I accepted the decision without kicking up a fuss. Whatever had made him this way wasn't something I had control over. I loved him in my way, though I was more and more detached. Mum couldn't contain her anger. She said he had some money that could make Theda's life easier, but we'd not seen any of it. Mum was broke because she had paid for all of Theda's care. It had caused a severe rift between her and Dad, more than their divorce ever had.

I was hardly in a better financial position than Mum. I had taken up the habit of blowing my savings every year on long trips to Asia to get a break from my life in Perth. I was struggling with the city on a few levels. I knew people, but I felt alone and misunderstood. Sojourning in Asia each year was part of what kept my spirits from falling too low, but it wasn't financially sensible.

I stayed in touch with Dad but was careful not to bring him up around Theda. She hadn't spoken to him for years, but after I told her he was leaving Perth she was upset. One time, when I knew he was returning to Perth for a few weeks (after he'd been away a year or so), I told Mum about it in the kitchen. Theda overheard, and just hearing that her father was returning but wasn't planning on seeing her triggered a psychosis.

Another time, when she was mildly psychotic but we'd caught it early and begun medicating, we tried admitting her to an unlocked ward. Her delusions weren't too bad that time, and she wasn't unmanageable. But a psychiatrist at the ward looked like our father, and she became fixated on the idea that he wanted to harm her. It sent her into a full-blown psychotic delusional state and she had to be sectioned.

Whatever our father meant to my sister, it was powerful.

★

It's not entirely accurate that Mum, Theda and I were the only family left in Perth after Dad had gone. Our father had a nephew living in Perth's outer suburbs. He was a young guy who'd fled Burma in the early 2000s, but our lack of a common language meant we didn't know how to share much. He worked at a factory with other Burmese refugees. I knew he cared about my mother and sister, but I wasn't sure if he understood what was happening. I saw him about once a year.

Mum dropped most of her social networks. Looking after Theda was exhausting, but she said the biggest burden was friends who didn't understand. They dismissed Theda's illness, telling Mum she was too soft and needed to push Theda harder. I understood this because I had experienced a version of it among my friends when I tried to share what was going on.

'Your sister sounds like she just needs to get out of bed,' one friend exclaimed when I tried to explain. I encountered too many responses like that, so I stopped trying to talk about it.

Theda had no social outlets. The friends she'd once made in university were getting on with their lives. Some occasionally stayed in touch via text message and email, but she couldn't speak on the phone or leave the house, nor could she use a computer much, so her replies were sporadic and it was pretty one-sided.

★

I found myself being a confidant and an adviser to Mum. I understood what her friends couldn't about Theda's illness. I tried encouraging her when I thought she might scale back something in Theda's care regime. I was occasionally dismissive of Dr Nihal's expertise when I felt I could get away with it. I was eager to discourage what I saw as excesses in his advice whenever I saw Mum waver enough to consider it that way. But I knew I risked showing my secret distrust of the M.E. diagnosis if I went too far. Mum and Theda were deeply bound up in each other's trauma, defined by that diagnosis, and they couldn't afford another dissenting family member.

'If it weren't for you, Khin,' Mum would say often, 'I would turn on the oven and close all the windows. It would put your sister and me out of our misery.'

I understood why my mother said this, but it affected me. On the one hand, she needed to express her despair somehow; on the other, saying it made me feel responsible for whether or not my family suicided.

As the years went by like this, I learned to dread my phone ringing. Most people texted, but when it rang Mum was usually the person on the other end. I also picked up calls from random numbers, just in case it was a hospital or the police. I was waiting for news of death or psychosis. If it wasn't bad news, it might be Mum asking me to come over so I could talk to my sister about not committing suicide. During those years, it felt like one wrong turn on my part might leave everyone dead. At the same time, I knew I was at odds with them and liable to make a wrong move because I doubted something at the core of the identity that they needed me to believe in.

It was around this time that I began to feel quite distant from my community in Fremantle. After Melbourne, I'd started over in Perth's so-called 'alternative' suburb. It was the equivalent of Fitzroy in Melbourne, privileged and progressive, but much smaller and with hippies. When I'd moved back, it had seemed like Perth presented only two options: hippies or bogans. I'd picked hippies because they seemed the non-macho option.

On the surface, hippy culture encouraged men to talk about their feelings. But as I got through my twenties, I started to see it differently. I couldn't see men relating to each other with much depth or vulnerability. The 'spiritual' language they used was a way of staying distant. Spiritual buzzwords fuelled hedonistic pursuits, which came at the expense of any genuine attempt at empathy or diversity. The local history of Fremantle centred around the Indian mystic Osho's followers, who had dropped out of the rat race to practise free love and dope smoking alongside meditation a generation earlier. They had been children of the '70s and so-called radicals, and their kids were often happily downwardly mobile. I mixed with those kids and they were friendly to me – my musical skills helped greatly as social lubricant – but as my family's troubles got more serious, I no longer felt connected to anyone. I mostly had female friends, but even so, they lived in a different universe from me.

Friends said I needed to learn detachment if I was upset about my family. If my sister was ill with something ambiguous, she most likely needed to work on herself. Fremantle was under the spell of the wellness industry, and if most medical professionals struggled to think outside a mind–body binary, the hippie subculture never failed to fuse the two things. Neither option was right.

In hippy discourse, conflating mind and body helps you blame a person's suffering on spiritual lack, which conveniently frees up your empathy reserves for festivals, hallucinogens, sleeping around and goddess rituals. There was an individualism at play, masquerading as communal soup kitchens, where white men with dreadlocks hit on white girls in cheesecloth.

Sometimes I made a friend whom I could relate to, but they always jumped ship and moved east, searching for a larger and more cosmopolitan place to live. I wished I could do the same, but I needed a better reason to leave. Theda was only getting sicker.

My job was the one thing I felt connected to outside my own family. I taught adult refugees English, and it kept me sane for a couple of reasons. One was that I got time off during the school holidays. Around December each year, I could jump on a plane to Asia. Classes didn't start again until February, and I would invariably start over again in Perth each time I returned, searching for a new group of friends who might understand me better. The other reason my job was fulfilling was that refugees constantly reminded me (inadvertently) that my troubles sat alongside many, often much more tragic, stories. All my colleagues were over sixty, but I liked them too. They were Christian ladies who'd joined the profession out of a sense of spiritual duty that was much more genuine than the Christian-hating wellness-industry spirituality of my social stamping ground.

I often felt the world wasn't quite real during this time. I can't wholly blame Perth or Fremantle, though I'd like to. My personality was a bit unstable. I was grumpy and easily put off things and people I didn't like the look of. Whatever the cause, I felt alone.

★

I stopped my role as Neo at some point during these years too. I remember the night it first happened. I was in an emergency ward. Mum was off with some doctors preparing paperwork to have Theda committed, and I was tasked with controlling Theda in the middle of a busy ER. She and I were sitting on a stretcher as she clanged away. I'd been anxious during the last couple of psychotic breaks because she had been aggressive towards Mum. I also knew that Mum would fight to get her out of the hospital too soon because she hated her being in those locked wards.

Something in me changed gears that day, because instead of leaning into her psychosis and talking to her about her delusions as if I also believed they might hold the key to something, I gently pushed against them.

I remember she looked at me like I was playing a game at first. 'See those people in beds?' I said. I was drawing her attention to the patients, hospital machinery and staff uniforms. 'Does it make sense that we are in a hospital?'

As I persisted, she looked unsure of herself. No one had ever managed to pull her out of psychosis before, so I didn't know if I would succeed, but for a moment I thought I saw recognition. 'You see the thing we're sitting on?' I said, touching the cold metal railing of the stretcher frame. 'You've had a psychosis. You're alright. There's nothing to be afraid of. It just happens sometimes.'

She looked at me and I saw she was back in reality. I took her hand, talking soothingly and assuring her she was safe. I looked away for a moment to find where our mother was, then I felt a thump on my back and turned. Her fist was balled and ready. 'You're one of them,' she spat.

★

The vast majority of my sister's time was not psychotic. And during those long swathes of bedridden sanity, her ability to communicate slowly deteriorated. She made more literal sense when she wasn't psychotic but constantly apologised because she was convinced she *wasn't* making sense.

There were only a few topics she could speak about without falling apart. Suicide was one of them. I became a good listener. And I had come to understand through talking to her and remembering my own suicidal thinking that discussing such thoughts is key to coping with them. Some think it's best not to talk about suicide lest it encourage action. Journalists, for example, follow rules not to cover suicide despite it being the leading cause of death for young people in a country like Australia. I don't agree with that approach because I don't think it works. Valorising suicide isn't the same as acknowledging the reality that suicidal thoughts exist for many of us. It doesn't even need a trigger warning in my opinion. In fact, the opposite is true. A society that pathologically refuses to talk about suicide despite the rising rates (and many citizens who struggle with compulsive suicidal thoughts) is what truly warrants a trigger warning. Treating suicide as a taboo topic made my sister's suicidal thoughts worse. Shame compounded them.

I could often make Theda laugh once she'd finished telling me about her persistent desire to die.

'I miss flavour,' she said once, after telling me how she hoped she'd die in her sleep. She was referring to the various diets that Dr Nihal and his specialists had her on.

'Which flavours?'

'All of them,' she said, grinning.

Mum often remarked on how I made my sister laugh when I visited. It was a privilege. I had been Neo during her psychotic breaks; I became the friend who could laugh at the ridiculous proposition of life alongside her when she was sane.

One year, a hospital pain clinic gave her fentanyl for her neuropathic pain. A few months in, she was vomiting several times a day and getting rashes from touching certain types of material.

Mum took her to Fremantle Hospital, and an expert there interpreted the new symptoms through the lens of his speciality. He sent her home, saying she had an acquired multiple chemical sensitivity syndrome. However, six weeks later she wasn't recovering, and Mum took her back. The doctor realised his mistake and immediately admitted her to a general ward, taking her off the fentanyl cold turkey, which spun her into psychosis.

Whatever else uncertain medical conditions do, they draw out people's inability to see the lenses through which they themselves view the world.

Nineteen

After a week in Syracuse, a woman messaged me on the dating website. I'd given up on anyone contacting me, because no one on that site was in the city, but I got a message in my email telling me I had a 'potential romance brewing'.

She lived in Ithaca, a town a couple of hundred miles south. I'd heard of Ithaca. Rachel had sung its praises once, and hoped we might live there when we were married and raising a family. It was a progressive university town. I'd never thought of rural towns as progressive, but Rachel had said it was both.

Patricia wrote that she was originally from Montreal. She described Ithaca as 'a little Portland' and told me I should come down and visit.

I'd often joked with Theda that heaven had no genders. It was an idea we'd come across in Buddhism. It always made me laugh to remember that Buddhists associated gender with suffering, because I agreed but didn't see heaven coming soon. That said, a post-relationship malaise was oddly like heaven. I was uninterested in sex and romance, and it was a relief. Maybe I was experiencing numbness rather than liberation. But either way it took the anxiety out of dating.

Patricia was a scientist at the university. After I replied, she said I should do more than just visit her town if I wasn't enjoying Syracuse much. She said it would be a good place for an Australian who wants to write. Her suggestion didn't seem anything but friendly and unconcerned that we may or may not end up dating. I felt I was being addressed as a human being rather than a man, which was odd given the context of our conversation. I realised that I'd felt conspicuously male since

Rachel's court action and hated it. I didn't want to be my gender.

Near the end of the week, I phoned Layla Galatas and told her that I could pay for the preliminary. I wouldn't be able to afford a trial, but I'd decided to use my credit card for the initial hearing. The fee would be $5000.

Aside from student loans, I'd never taken on debt before. My card had an eight-thousand-dollar limit, but I had never let it go even ten dollars over. That was my one sensible financial habit. I remember that as I decided to let it happen for the first time it felt distinctly American. Less cautious people than me used their credit cards to pay lawyers when they didn't have a job. It was bold. It was also the only choice I could see in front of me. And it felt like the world was taunting me, challenging me to show it that I, too, could 'be a fucking man' as Rachel had demanded I do at the start of this whole episode.

★

In the evening, I knocked on Michael's bedroom door to tell him I was leaving Syracuse. After spending five thousand dollars on the lawyer, I figured it didn't matter if I also forewent the remaining rent I would lose if I left early.

When he greeted me at his bedroom door, he surprised me by inviting me in instead of chatting in the corridor. 'Do you want to see some photos of my birthday party?' he said.

I told him I did. He'd invited me to the celebration a couple of days earlier, but I'd sidestepped it. I figured it was polite at least to look at some photos.

He already had them in a physical album. It made me feel uneasy for some reason, as though he were a vulnerable person who needed reassurance. His friends looked dowdy and dull. He'd written 'Fortieth Birthday 2013' under each photograph. I felt neediness emanating from him, and I wondered if he'd invited me to the celebration because I represented a sense of adventure he'd not been able to have in his own life.

If only he knew how badly this 'adventure' was going.

'You don't have to worry about the money,' he said when I told him I was going. 'I'll give you a refund for the days you won't stay.'

I thanked him profusely and felt guilty for judging him.

'All that matters', he said, 'is that you're happy, Khin.'

★

The next day, as he drove me down to the bus station, he talked about how his sister had recently recovered from cancer. He'd looked after her kids while she'd gone through chemotherapy. The family was going through some troubles, which was why they were all together. I realised that I hadn't questioned why they were all living together.

'It's hard to date,' he said, 'living with your mother and sister. People judge you for it. But family matters, Khin. Family is the most important thing.'

I told him it was admirable that he'd sacrificed his needs for his sister, and for the first time I felt ashamed for having left mine back in Perth to come here.

He shrugged it off. 'That's just what family does.'

He then told a story that made me realise he had been watching me more closely than I'd thought. It was about a friend who'd got involved with a troubled woman. The woman sounded like a certain type as he described her. He said she was very attractive and emotionally 'intense'.

'This woman – we could all see she had issues. I'm surprised it lasted as long as it did. Everyone in our group warned him she was trouble.'

'What kind of trouble?' I asked.

He furrowed his brow and sighed. 'Just the kind that you see. Anyway, Greg didn't want to hear it. She was exciting, you know? Don't get me wrong. I'm not saying that she wasn't a good person – I'm sure she was – but she had mental health problems. And when she got a restraining order on him it really messed with his life.'

I suddenly felt conspicuous.

'A restraining order?' I asked, trying not to sound anxious.

Michael acted as if he didn't notice the tension in my voice. 'Who knows what goes on in people's relationships,' he said. 'But Greg was the one who broke it up. She wanted to get back together, and it wasn't until she realised he wouldn't do it that she called the cops and said he was stalking her. The police came into his work. It wasn't good for him. He was a contractor, you see – a wedding photographer – and they came to one of the weddings he was shooting to warn him not to contact her. It didn't look good at all. They revisited him two years later, at work again, just before the restraining order was due to expire, and warned him away. He said he hadn't even thought of contacting her, but they told him they were just doing their jobs.'

'And you're sure he hadn't done anything?' I asked.

He frowned. 'Look, you never know what's happening in someone else's relationship. But we saw it at the beginning – she was messed up. You gotta stay away from messed-up people, Khin. If you don't, they'll mess *you* up, and there's nothing you can do about it then. That's why it's best to just stay away from messed-up people.'

As I pondered the stress he was putting on the phrase 'messed up', I realised he had told me this story because he'd heard me talking on the phone in my room. It made sense since we had an adjoining door. He had invited a stranger into his home, only to overhear that stranger talking to lawyers and his mother about a sick sibling with a euthanasia drug and his own trouble with the law. And instead of judging me, he had felt pity. He recognised that the main thing I was grappling with was shame, and he was telling me this story so I didn't have to feel so monstrous with it.

Even as he offered empathy, I felt I didn't deserve it. And my instinct to believe the woman was so strong that I couldn't stop myself from asking one more time if Greg had done something. 'That sounds like it was tough for him,' I said eventually, though my sympathy was muted. I wondered if others would feel that way about me. Men stalked women;

everyone knew it. If some supposedly innocent man got caught up in the mechanisms of battling the broader social issue, so be it.

I also wondered if I was attracted to superficial people. Maybe I didn't gauge character as well as I thought. Maybe it was time I questioned why I'd been so attracted to Rachel's personality, and why I'd dismissed someone like Michael so readily. That was what my mother was saying – that I hadn't ever seen Rachel for who she was.

A few minutes later, we pulled into the coach-station car park. When my suitcase was on the curb, Michael shook my hand and pointed at a building over the road. 'That's Destiny,' he said. 'That's just the back of part of it – it's the largest shopping mall in New York State right there, Khin.' He jerked his head in the direction he was pointing to ensure I looked properly. There was pride in his voice. 'The whole thing is massive,' he said. 'They have a full-sized rollercoaster inside. Not just one of those small rollercoasters – you get those in some other malls – but a proper full-sized one. *Destiny, USA.*'

'Nice,' I said, unsure of what else I was expected to say. It seemed like another moment of perfect American cliché, like the billboard advertising a gun shop.

He smiled and nodded. 'Maybe you can see it next time you're in town.'

★

After he was gone, I thought about messed-up people. 'Messed-up' was so ambiguous. I didn't have a typical story – did that make me messed up? Early in my relationship with Rachel, when we met in Thailand, she'd complained that her life was overprotected and lacking adventure. She talked about dating a petty criminal before meeting me. She talked about dating a black guy and finding the supposed cultural difference too much. She talked about sophisticated ideas and knew things that Australia wouldn't hear about for another five years. But maybe she was a bit of a tourist. My life had intrigued her until it had become clearer that my financial circumstances might be an obstacle. She loved asking me about my life's experiences, but it was she who had the better education. That was ultimately the attitude of a tourist, wasn't it? I didn't see that as messed up while being on the receiving end of her interest. But nor was I convinced that Rachel hadn't actually loved me. She'd been vulnerable around me. She had told me many times that the things she'd shared with me about her deeper anxieties and mental health were things she'd never shared with anyone before.

Another thing to consider about Michael's advice was that I might never have got better if key people I'd met along the way had avoided me after my suicide attempts. My 'messed-up' soul had been evident to anyone with a pair of eyes who'd glanced at my wrist and seen the scars. Those scars were still obvious nearly twenty years later, but back when I was younger they were angry, raised and purple. I'd had people judge me because of them, but some people had taken chances on me and others had opened up in ways they wouldn't have otherwise. I'd healed because those people connected with what was messed up in me. Just as Michael had been kind in trying to make me feel better.

I sat down and waited for my ride.

Twenty

The year I turned thirty, I blew my savings and travelled to India on a six-month hiatus. I'd met an Irishwoman who wanted to go back to the subcontinent after her first visit, and she asked me to go with her. She was fascinating and I'd always wanted to see India.

'Go,' Mum said. 'Enjoy your life. We will be fine.'

India was different from what I expected. I'd seen poverty in Asia, but Indian poverty was at another level. People were so packed together, and their quick march towards death spilled onto the streets in ways I hadn't imagined.

My first jolt was on the taxi drive to my hotel. A truck boomed past with its driver atop a plastic chair, held in place by three metal poles welded over the exposed engine. There was no cabin around the driver, and not only did that look incredibly dangerous, but the pollution on the road was like soup. The stick-thin truck driver was hauling eighteen wheels behind him with nothing but a cloth around his nose and ski goggles for a windscreen.

Later, in the streets, amputees who looked like they wouldn't last more than another year dragged themselves around on flattened cardboard boxes. Children without eyes begged, and women passed babies around on the corner, pinching them to make them cry for the pedestrians up the road so that both babies and pseudo-mothers could eat. Police beat people with wooden sticks and no one batted an eyelid.

After a couple of months, I was in love with the Irishwoman. She'd grown up in the ghettos in Dublin and was suffering some kind of developmental trauma. Her mother had neglected her and her brother was in jail. She was unusual among backpackers. She was more used to the darker side of life, and she was hurt. She was distrustful. But she had a talent that made people like her and want her around. When she told me that she loved me back, she said she was angry about it. She said she felt more understood than she ever had with a guy, but she didn't really believe that men were capable of love so it made her vulnerable.

I didn't know how to respond to that, so I just left it and kept loving her. One of the other backpackers whom we got to know over several weeks said to me in private, 'Khin, I get why you love Rose. She's like the sun – everyone wants to be around her – but I pity you being so close.'

Another thing Rose could do was quell packs of stray dogs. In a country like India, that is a useful skill, and I learned from watching how she did it. It was the same magical manoeuvre she used on eager backpacker men who tried it on in the tourist bars. She mocked them but never too much. Something about her own struggles in life made her see their vulnerability while also handling how this manifested as arrogance. She had a soft spot for creatures that seemed vulnerable. I think that's why she liked me. I didn't feel vulnerable, but she said I was. Two arrogant Israeli backpackers once told her they didn't know why someone as sexy as her would choose a lover like me. She reported this to me and said the guys were idiots, but I understood their point.

She privately told me that she forgave Indian men when they tried to grope her. 'I get it,' she said, 'I'm this white girl in her twenties travelling around their country for months without working, when most of them work seven days a week and won't ever have the money to leave India. It's like I'm some figure from the movies taunting them. They hate me as much as they're attracted to me.' That was Rose – she saw her privilege as relative, while being less fortunate than many. It was a very attractive combination.

She was also a functioning alcoholic who held herself together until we were in private. We stayed in one town in the foothills of the Himalayas for a couple of months and she'd get abusive drunk each night. She was fine at the bar, but once we were in our room she would lay into me. She said once she felt like 'one of those husbands who hurts his partner each evening then begs forgiveness in the morning'. It wasn't physical violence, but she would hurl brutal, foul-mouthed insults at me. She said I should leave her because even when she apologised in the morning she knew she'd do it again.

The problem was that I felt understood by Rose. She intuited me somehow.

'I love your beautiful brown skin,' she said on the ghats in Udaipur once. It was the first time anyone had said something like that to me. Until that point in my life, I'd only ever dated white girls who'd said the opposite. They didn't mean to be racist, but they all used the same phrase, 'You're not like other Asians; I don't usually find Asian men attractive.' In my mind, that had always been a compliment because it meant I was doing my job of passing as white very well. But Rose understood me better than I understood myself on that level.

We danced a strange dance over the six months we backpacked the subcontinent. I tried to leave her once, and she clawed at my clothes, begging me not to. I abandoned her in the end for a reason she probably never understood.

We almost made it to Europe, where we intended to start a new life together. She didn't want to go back to Ireland, and I had a British passport thanks to Mum's nationality – so we thought about Belgium. Mum gave me her blessing to leave Perth permanently and start a new life. Mum had been passing my messages on to Theda and said my sister (too ill to use a phone) understood why I needed to go if I was in love.

An email came about a week after Rose and I had made definite plans. Mum emailed on Theda's behalf and asked me to call because Theda wanted to talk.

When I heard my sister's voice on the phone, it was raspy. 'Minty?' she said. 'How's India?'

'I've lost a lot of weight from food poisoning,' I joked.

I was sitting at a stall overlooking the ocean from a cliffside.

I looked down at my feet. They were dirty. A few weeks earlier, Rose had said that backpacking India was a cruise ship for people who couldn't afford a cruise, and I had realised I was tired of it.

'Did Mum tell you about the book?' she said.

I told her yes.

'It's time we start considering that I won't get better.'

There was a tiredness in her voice beyond whatever fatigue she felt that day. It was the weariness of someone who has faced a question they wanted to avoid and come up with the answer they had been most afraid was true, then had the unforgiving task of finding their footing and needing to tell it to people.

'It talks about euthanasia, right?'

'It says you should ask your loved ones for permission.'

'It's not my choice,' I said haltingly.

'We've tried everything. I just want to know that it's okay with you if I do decide to go.'

I stared at the ocean. Little waves were cresting at the shoreline below, and I thought of how nature sets its own timeline. Mum had done all the work of explaining the situation in her email, but Theda wanted to ask me the question herself.

We chatted for a while longer. And she said she wanted her death to be gentle if it came. I realised that I could make her feel less horrible about having such a thought in one's thirties. She said it wasn't something she was considering this month, or even this year. But she wanted to know if it was okay for some indefinite time in the future if that came to pass.

I couldn't give her my blessing explicitly, because the words wouldn't form in my mouth, but I told her that I had never asked permission before my suicide attempts and didn't believe it was anyone's right to make such a decision except the person facing it.

I told her I loved her.

When I went back to the hut that night, Rose was drunk and angry. She said it sounded like my sister just wanted attention and needed to be forced to get up out of bed. Despite her insightfulness, Rose couldn't ever make sense of my sister's illness, so I'd avoided talking about it much until then. I wasn't angry, but I realised I wouldn't be moving to Europe after that conversation. It took me a while to let Rose know that, perhaps because I didn't want to admit it to myself, either.

When she left Delhi on a plane to Belgium, the plan was that I would meet her in a month's time in Brussels. But I returned to Perth instead.

When I got back to Australia, it felt like I had gone backwards. I didn't know where to start in my social life, so I started over again with a new cluster of friends who weren't as hippy as my last lot. I briefly dated a woman. One evening, she came to my house after an environmental protest wearing only body paint and panties. She was so pleased with herself. We inadvertently crossed paths with my mother later that day. It was the first time the two of them had met, and Mum began talking about wanting to commit suicide in the first two minutes. It was awkward, and I understood that. But when that woman I was dating talked about how 'weird' it was afterwards, the rising intonation at the end of her statements made her sound like a teenager, and I lost my attraction to her. There were no Roses in my new social milieu.

This was the year people around me began joining Facebook. I was surprised when Mum made Theda a Facebook account. She said it was good for keeping in 'contact' with Theda's old university friends, and Mum checked the account regularly on my sister's behalf, sending out friend requests and reporting back if one was accepted.

A man Theda had known while doing her broadcasting course many years earlier got in touch. He messaged, asking what she was doing in the industry. He assumed she was working because she'd been at the top of their class, and he was shocked to find she'd got sick just before her final assignment – an internship in Sydney – and never even finished. Mum explained it all to him in a message.

Another development involved a Belgian specialist whom Dr Nihal had told us to contact. The Belgian was an M.E. expert who was visiting and giving a lecture in Perth. It would be costly to arrange a home visit but possible, and this man could offer treatment avenues that we hadn't tried yet.

When I opened the door, the Belgian introduced himself and shook my hand with a handshake so faint it was memorable. He was short and spongy-looking, wearing loose-fitting beige pants and a clean white shirt. Part of what made his handshake memorable was the skin on his palm and fingers. It was so soft that it made me think of rich creams in little tubs.

'I'll see the patient,' he said, in an accent between Dutch and French.

He headed to my sister's bedroom while Mum and I waited in the kitchen. When he returned twenty minutes later, he declared my sister was suffering from the worst case of myalgic encephalomyelitis he'd ever seen. He said we needed to prepare her for a medicine called Gc-MAF that could cure her.

'We take a dual approach,' he said. 'The gut is the key. Gc-MAF will cure her, but her body won't absorb it until we prepare the gut. Ideally, we get her a direct line for feeding. I sell nutritional supplements.'

He didn't say Gc-MAF *might* cure her. He spoke as if it was definite and a pity that we hadn't ever encountered such an obvious solution. He talked about Australia being far behind Europe when it came to accepting and treating M.E., which he assured us had no links to the mind or trauma.

When Mum asked what 'a direct line for feeding' was, he explained that it was a tube that would pump nutrition directly into my sister's stomach, requiring surgery for the installation.

He then explained that the nutritional supplements we needed could only be sourced from his practice in Belgium. We'd need to have them shipped over. The Gc-MAF would be more difficult because it wasn't approved for use in Australia, so technically it wasn't legal to ship here. We would have to order it, but the company sending it wouldn't be able to ensure it arrived and we'd take that risk. They would use a nondescript box. He said it was unlikely we'd have issues, because he knew other Australian families who'd done the same. But it wasn't cheap. When he told us the price – a thousand dollars per month – I saw Mum's neck muscles move.

After he was gone, she talked about remortgaging her home. I pleaded with her not to. Having the mortgage paid off was the only lucky thing about this situation.

'Getting her better is all that matters,' Mum said.

'Yes, but where will you live?' I asked.

She looked worried and then talked about my father in unflattering terms.

★

Mum was adamant we'd find a way to afford Gc-MAF. The nutritional supplements would also be five hundred dollars per month, which meant fifteen hundred dollars every four weeks. No one except Dad might have been able to afford that.

Mum refused to ask Dad because she'd asked and been rejected before. It hurt too much, she said. But when my sister's old university friend contacted her Facebook account, he asked if we'd talk to the press about my sister's illness to raise awareness about just how bad the situation was for people with chronic fatigue. The timing coincided with our desperate need for money, and I think Mum thought it could also help us personally. Perhaps she believed the government might make Gc-MAF a Medicare-subsidised medicine in the timeframe we needed, and as unrealistic as that may have been we didn't have other options. So that is how we let the press into our lives.

★

It was small-scale at first. Theda's old university friend worked for the ABC, and he connected us to a former colleague who now wrote for an online publication. A reporter came to the house with a photographer, and the story appeared on the publication's website a few days later.

I didn't know that people were reading and sharing news online, but they were. Theda's story caught fire. It went viral. Suddenly all the major TV news networks were calling us. They produced shows that aired directly after the nightly news, focusing on current affairs and human interest, often lampooned by media-savvy comedians for their sensationalism. But no one in my family had much media literacy, nor were we in a position to be picky. I didn't properly understand those shows, but I knew they focused on bully/victim stories. And Theda's was a story where the mainstream medical establishment could be cast as the bully.

Mum asked me to help her on the day the journalists arrived. I got there at lunchtime to find three vans with different logos painted on their sides parked on her front lawn.

There was a journalist in the kitchen talking to Mum when I entered the house. 'Doctors don't believe in M.E.,' she was telling him. 'The government won't let medicines like Gc-MAF into Australia because they don't believe it's a real illness.'

The journalist shook his head. 'That's awful,' he said.

He said he wanted an interview with Theda, but Mum told him Theda couldn't handle the lighting and stress. I wondered if Theda could even string a sentence together. Her brain fog meant I was lucky if even I could talk to her on some days.

'People need to *see* your daughter,' the journalist said. 'We can do it in low light. We'll just get her voice and the outline of her.'

When Mum explained that one interview might be okay but there were two other news crews on the front lawn, the journalist asked if we could wait while he problem-solved. He went outside and returned five minutes later, saying all the channels had agreed to share raw footage, which meant Theda could do one interview and each channel would then separately interview my mother so that once the stories were edited together they wouldn't look like copies. It meant they could play on competing networks without issue.

'The world needs to know,' the journalist told my mother in a soothing voice. 'Not just for your daughter, but for other people *like* her.' His charisma was unshakable, and he had the kind of intelligence you wanted to trust because it seemed warm and sincere.

A week later, the segments aired across three networks simultaneously. It was so well-timed that you couldn't have flicked from one channel to another without seeing my sister's shadowy outline as she attempted to talk to a journalist for a few minutes. I was glad the story didn't question the diagnosis. They didn't mention her psychotic breaks. Nor did they mention anything else that could cast doubt on the clean idea that M.E. was a well-understood physical illness that the conservative medical establishment refused to take seriously. My uncertainties aside, Theda didn't need more shame. She didn't need a nation of malleable TV viewers suspecting that she was undeserving of sympathy.

I still had mixed feelings about the coverage because it solidified certainty within my family around the M.E. diagnosis. The segments made no mention of heterogeneous patient groups, competing diagnoses, major medical bodies stating that the causes of M.E. were unknown, or potentially charlatan doctors pushing dangerous treatments.

The Gc-MAF didn't get named – most likely for legal reasons – and instead, narrating journalists talked about 'medicines that could cure people like Theda Myint'. They were medicines the Australian government refused to allow or cover costs for. The bully/victim set-up was in that arrangement of facts.

After airing their segments, producers from two channels called my mother saying they were overwhelmed by viewers phoning in to thank them because they had family members in a similar plight. These journalists wanted to interview us again in six months and told us that some viewers also wanted to make donations.

I felt conflicted because my mother was saved from remortgaging her home but any hope of our reconsidering the diagnosis was vanishing. The TV narrative made a black-and-white division between mental and physical diseases stronger in the name of protecting the vulnerable, which made questioning it harder. That narrative cast doubters as victim blamers, even though such a rigid and false division potentially made things worse for the people suffering. In short, the media narrative was meant to open people's minds, but it implicitly increased the stigma around illnesses that didn't neatly fit the mental–physical disease binary.

I began paying attention to what was happening on Facebook. Initially, people had shared the text story about my sister, and now videos of her interview went global among specific networks. Those networks were online communities for M.E. sufferers and their families, and I joined out of solidarity but was often troubled by what I saw. There was a lot of personal storytelling that seemed supportive, and members who'd been suffering for years with disbelieving doctors. They expressed their shame and humiliation in ways that seemed to foster solidarity and healing. But on the other hand, amateur health advice was rampant. People shared symptom lists that were so long and diverse they could have captured any number of illnesses; you only needed to tick a few in order to belong. And the treatment ideas shared were from various corners of the globe and internet. People also shared lists of 'M.E.-literate' doctors around the world who viewed the disease as entirely physical.

I hit the 'like' button on some of the storytellers' posts because I cared about the community, but I was unsure what to think about the fact that they were online echo chambers. Any dissent was quickly shut down, and people suggesting M.E. had mental health links, in terms of either cause or treatment possibilities, were called victim blamers outright. Any uncertainty was eschewed.

I would one day find a way of seeing a historical context for this hard division between mind and body in medicine. It was the philosopher

Descartes who created the mind–body split in philosophy. He did it by rebranding the *soul* as the mind.

Before Descartes, early medicine had tied some diseases to moral judgements about the soul. Mental and psychosomatic disorders were routinely categorised as signs of internal ethical corruption, and you could hang a witch in the European Middle Ages on that basis. Psychosomatic medical conditions fared worst of all and were the cause of the Salem witch trials. A doctor noted medically unexplainable symptoms in a group of highly repressed young women in Puritan New England and referred them to a priest, who explained their symptoms as God's punishment for witchcraft.

When Descartes said *cogito ergo sum* (I think, therefore I am), he replaced the idea of the soul as our essential self with the idea of a thinking creature – a mind – that defined our essence. Psychiatry emerged as physicians took note and declared the mind worthy of study in the same way the body was studied. This gave birth to the modern idea of mental illness.

Rebranding the *soul* as the *mind* didn't shake off millennia of cultural prejudice, however. People with mental illnesses weren't hanged, but they were still thrown into asylums and branded lunatics. They were 'treated', but general acceptance and sympathy for their suffering wasn't forthcoming. A change in vocabulary was a gentrification rather than a real revolution. Perhaps it was an early example of politically correct language failing to elicit the promised change. The profound issue was not wording but knowledge itself and how it was structured. Changing the label but retaining the binary opposition as the undergirding for separate institutions, with their patients given different levels of respect, proved to be an issue. As a more contemporary philosopher – Derrida – pointed out, when you have a binary, one side usually gets the better deal. That's how power distribution gets woven into knowledge itself. Division is the fundamental manoeuvre of thought – division separates *this* from *that*. What we fail to note is how dignity and privilege are bonded to the result.

Society fears examining its knowledge structures. In particular, people don't like recognising that scientific knowledge is part of a larger subjective project in which value is assigned according to who is in charge. Medical knowledge is rife with ambiguities, and there is always a favoured group within the current set-up, but drawing attention to that is often met with collective denial. Psychiatrists might have been novel when they first appeared in history, but they were also suspect; doctors – who treated the body – had been worthy of respect as healers since the beginning. Doctors treated *us*. Psychiatry treated *them*. Medicine was determined to view a human being as a two-part thing.

★

As the media got involved in our family story, I couldn't label a feeling I was having. It felt as though a wall had appeared. It was muddy glass separating two very different worlds – me and everything else. A lot of my new friends mentioned having seen Theda on TV. I tried to explain my concerns to a couple of them. 'But isn't it a real illness?' they asked.

Earlier that decade, friends and acquaintances had been inclined to victim blaming. Now they thought I was blaming my sister's illness on her. All I wanted was some company with the uncertainty I was facing. Dad was gone, and Mum and Theda were convinced that her illness was a marginalised physical condition. Their doctors and the media agreed. So I was out on a limb with my doubts. And yet I couldn't forget them.

Sometimes, after leaving my mother's house, I would shake. I was splitting apart but couldn't tell anyone because there was no language to describe why.

★

Who magazine contacted us shortly after the TV stories and did a two-page feature. Donations had come in after the TV coverage, giving us enough to try Gc-MAF. When that didn't work, Mum used the leftover money to buy a bathtub because soaking in warm water helped my sister's neuropathic pain. Mum also purchased a solid wood door to more or less soundproof Theda's bedroom. And she bought a humidity-controlling air conditioner. These salves for Theda's symptoms were sensible, and I was grateful that my sister had meaning again. She talked about being part of something larger than herself because others might benefit from her sharing her story.

'Even if I never get better,' she told me. 'At least I can be part of something that helps others.'

Twenty-One

'Denver is where it's at,' the stocky man in the pale blue shirt said as he drove. It was mid-afternoon and buildings were thinning out and slowly being replaced by greenery as we headed down a highway towards Ithaca.

I felt relief at leaving Syracuse. Michael had been nice, and it wasn't a terrible city, but I was glad not to be returning. The car I was in was an old Lincoln Town Car from the '70s (my driver had informed me about it in great detail when I'd asked). Its leather seats looked worn and cared for.

'I mean, you can gamble on the Oswego,' he continued, thick hands on the wheel. 'Chicago is good as well. But I go to Denver.'

'What's good about Denver?' I asked.

'Bigger,' he said. 'What happens in Denver *stays* in Denver.' He chuckled and touched his nose before putting both hands firmly back in place.

I'd booked a car because there didn't seem to be any bus service connecting the two cities. This was meant to be a minibus service, but the driver had arrived in the sedan, saying that no one else was travelling that day. He was in his fifties and everything about him said working class to me. His trousers looked like what you would find in an op shop, but if I were to guess I would say he'd bought them in the '70s and had taken good care of them. His personality was comforting but unusual. It took me a while to realise it was because he was a white man doing a manual job with a gentle talkativeness about him. Back home in Perth, I never encountered that mix of qualities.

'Do you only drive this route?' I asked.

'Not in July,' he said. 'Students are on holiday. Not many people go to Ithaca this time of year.'

'What's the university called?'

'You probably mean Cornell,' he said. 'They have Ithaca College too. That's a good school, but Cornell is the famous one.'

The scene outside turned into a birch forest and our conversation flowed over topics in a casual way. I had been pretty alone since leaving Albany, and I was enjoying talking. We spoke about the Native American reservations and their casinos, American football and the importance of college sports in US culture. He wanted to know if Australia had a national sport and I tried to explain AFL.

'It's a bit like a mixture between basketball and rugby,' I said.

He laughed, probably imagining something wildly different. It was funny; I rarely felt like an Australian back home, but I often did abroad. People heard my accent and it was the most obvious thing about me, whereas back home no one noticed an Australian accent so instead they noticed the colour of my skin.

The rest of the drive was rolling hills beyond a plain. We passed a small lake with houses dotted around it. A few had small jetties with little rowboats attached. Something about the scene made me feel nostalgic. My travels in Asia had always been arresting because life was so different there, but American life was much closer to Australian life and culture, and created deja vu. The familiarity was just offbeat enough to awaken some dreamy part of your mind. I thought of Michael and his perfect grooming, Layla Galatas and her hooked nose and shoulder-padded skirt suit. There was something about this that made me feel a different person, a better version of myself, a happier and more coherent creature. I was calmer than I had been in a long time.

Perth machismo and its fragmented stoicism wasn't here.

At one point, my driver told a story about having owned a company with more cars. He'd employed a mechanic who left a welder on that started a fire. All the cars were lost and insurance didn't cover it. When I asked if there was a court case about it, he just looked surprised and said accidents happen.

After that, our conversation lulled and the hills shifted back. A forest swept up and we slowed down as the road curved and the sunlight turned green.

★

When we reached Ithaca, I said goodbye and he dropped me by a cluster of restaurants with young people sitting at outside tables. I wheeled my suitcase along a sidewalk, and an attractive woman smiled at me and unexpectedly said, 'Welcome!' My first thought was that she'd mistaken me for someone else, then I remembered that I had a suitcase with me and probably looked like a student who'd just arrived in a college town. It felt like a good omen.

On the way to my Airbnb, I walked past two churches. One had a rainbow flag on its archway and the other had *All Faiths Welcome* on a placard by its door. A residential house one block north had Tibetan prayer flags strung over the deck and a noticeboard informing people about weekly meditations and some nuns on a trip to India.

When I reached where I was staying, there was a small gorge that ran the length of a laneway beside the house. It was a creek with vertical rocky sides sunk a few metres below street level. Houses either side faced each other with unfenced flowering front gardens, and it made me think of something Rachel had said once about Perth and its habit of fencing in front yards, as though the people in the houses were afraid of each other. 'You live in one of the safest places in the world and people do that!' she'd cried.

I peered down into the running water. A slim diamond-headed snake wove its way between some reeds before disappearing.

I stepped up onto the deck and knocked on the door.

Twenty-Two

A few months after the media stories broke, Mum called and said we had another psychosis on our hands.

When I arrived, my sister's room was full of sunlight. She was sitting cross-legged on her bed with the curtains open and a wild look in her eyes. Random objects were strewn around. Mum stayed in the kitchen to call the paramedics. She hadn't wanted to call them until I was there, afraid of how my sister might react because she'd been threatening towards Mum earlier.

'Neo!' Theda shouted with glee when she saw me.

I saw that the wardrobe was open and her childhood dolls were out, which often happened when these 'visitors' took up residence in her. The room was messy, with objects in odd places. Some old photos and clothes from when she'd been well were on the bed.

She started talking about the Egyptians, and I decided to engage.

'You mean in a past life?' I asked.

'Oh, you know about the Egyptians!' she said, rolling her eyes dramatically and nodding. Suddenly everything on her face dropped and she was no longer present. Tears spilled down her cheeks as if she'd already been crying and I'd only just noticed. Her chin trembled and she was angry. 'We should have *said*. I couldn't ... And – Oh God! – and *Gemma!*' She was sobbing now. 'They *raped* us, Neo. They raped Gemma *first* to make me watch. And then me. Then they buried us. They buried us in the ground and I could see Gemma was still alive.' Her face screwed up and she was shaking her head. 'So was I,' she whispered. 'They said that room was *exclusive*. But we had every right to—'

She lifted her eyes and looked at me. 'No!' she screamed.

With remarkable speed and strength, she flew off the bed at me and shoved me backwards. I regained my balance and went after her, but she was already halfway down the hallway. She'd picked something up as she'd gone past me, and when I caught up with her inside the kitchen door she was launching at our mother with the object above her head. We tumbled into the bookcase, and whatever was in her hands crashed onto the tiles as she began to shriek. I held her down while Mum stood staring at us with a phone in one hand by the kitchen counter.

I began to worry about Mum's safety after that day. When Theda was safely in a locked ward, Mum and I pieced together what had happened. Theda had grabbed a large crystal, roughly the size of a football, from her bedside table. It was a rose quartz someone from one of the online M.E. groups had sent her – at least a few kilograms heavy, which was ironic because when not psychotic she could barely lift a fork. While recounting that story about the priests, she'd likely heard Mum speaking to paramedics on the phone in the kitchen and muddled the two things. That was the nature of psychosis: source monitoring malfunctioned, and contexts and emotions got jumbled up. My sister experienced paramedics as evildoers when she was psychotic – all she usually understood was that they were trying to take her away and restrain her against her will. I guess it was close to the trauma she was remembering (or reliving or imagining). Rape, murder, a person calling paramedics – it had all mushed into one and she'd attacked. She would likely have killed our mother in her deranged state if I hadn't been there.

Twenty-Three

Patricia had a pretty face. She was slightly chubby with fine blonde hair and inquisitive blue eyes.

'Syracuse isn't nice, is it?' she said.

I laughed and she smiled coyly. I realised that this quietly self-assured person was at least a little bit interested in me. It didn't mean much, only that she might be a new friend and wasn't put off by the look of me or how I'd ordered our coffees. It was her lunch break, which cordoned off the date nicely so we wouldn't have to spend too much time together if we didn't like each other.

'I've never been to a college town,' I said. 'We don't have them in Australia.'

'It's so cool', she said, 'that you're from *Ahs-traylia!*'

After that, we chatted and it felt friendly. I didn't expect her to be interested in me once she got to know me. I'd never felt that highly educated women found me very attractive. I felt underinformed in their presence. Rachel had been the first well-read and highly ambitious woman who'd ever shown interest. But Patricia was polite. She told me that she was a scientist doing something called a postdoc at Cornell. She told me a little about her previous partner, and when I asked if she'd been single long she said it had only been about six months. She described him and it sounded to me like he'd been depressed, but she called it lacking motivation. I told her that I wasn't accomplished, but instead of frowning at this she seemed to warm to me. 'I just like people who are trying to do something,' she said. 'It doesn't need to be some big accomplishment.'

I shrugged in embarrassment.

'You want to be a writer, right? Did you know that Nabokov wrote *Lolita* here?'

'Really?'

She nodded. 'Have you read it?'

'I've seen the movie,' I said.

'Nabokov worked at Cornell, and he took buses around town and listened in on schoolgirls having conversations so he could get Lolita's voice right.'

I was impressed, and she seemed pleased. I was glad to be part of that pleasure.

After coffee, she left me on the lawn outside the university library with instructions to explore the campus because I'd need 'places to hang out and write', and the campus was a good pick. 'It's interesting here,' she said. 'We have people from all over the world, though I don't think I've met any other Australians yet.'

★

I spent the rest of the day exploring Ithaca. The settlement was arranged into two hubs – Collegetown and downtown – and you could walk between them. In fact, everything was within walking distance. The place was like a large country town, with lots of trees and gorges and parks. The gorges cracked the landscape mysteriously. Roads were built around them, sometimes bridging the littler ones. I was intrigued by the conversations I overheard. There was an unusual mix of people around. I recognised the American version of hippies sitting in the parks with guitars. They had colourful clothing and seemed not to care about whiling away an afternoon. But there were also academics, and I overheard one man talking about a particle collider up on the campus while he was waiting in line at the grocery store. Later that afternoon, I saw a woman hauling fertiliser into the back of her ute. She was wearing gumboots and stopped to chat with an older man about some pigs that were having piglets.

In the evening, I texted Patricia to thank her and she texted straight back, suggesting we see each other again the next day. We made plans to meet at a place on campus.

The following day, I walked up the hill. I found her just outside the cafe, but instead of going inside, she offered to show me around. It was bigger than any campus I'd ever been on. A mixture of old stone buildings and new ones dotted large lawns and courtyards that were crisscrossed with paths and people sitting in groups. She told me it was usually busier, but that most of the students were on summer break. Apparently, Ithaca's population doubled or tripled when the students were in town.

I kissed her lightly on the lips as we parted ways and she seemed pleased about it.

She texted that evening and asked if I wanted to go to her house for dinner the next night.

★

When I arrived, she was wearing a pretty blue pinafore and smelled very faintly of perfume. She showed me around her tiny subdivided wood-frame house. We kissed for a moment on the couch before she asked me up to her bedroom. When we were in bed, I remembered Rachel's comments about wanting a rougher lover. They nagged for a moment, then I pushed them away. The sex was nice. Patricia came, and I figured she wanted me to feel good and faked it or she came easily. I didn't, but she didn't seem to mind. Afterwards, she went downstairs to prepare dinner, saying it was funny how we'd fallen into bed before eating.

I remember feeling cosy in her bed by myself. She'd cleaned her sheets and I could smell the washing powder and sunlight on them. Leonard Cohen was playing downstairs, and his woody baritone wafted up as I listened to Patricia banging pots in her tiny kitchen. I felt unhitched in a way that reminded me of a time I had paraglided in India, strapped to an instructor, in an almost silent and unexpectedly cocoon-like experience that felt both comfortable and freeing at the same time.

★

The next day, I emailed the owner of my Airbnb to ask about renting a room long-term. The rental arrangement was odd because the house's tenants didn't choose who took the upstairs bedrooms via the Airbnb website, and the owner didn't live on the property. It meant that Airbnb guests shared permanent tenants' living spaces downstairs without those tenants having any say in it. I'd spoken to all three women staying there, and they'd all said it would be a relief if a long-term tenant took the room.

When the owner arrived, I saw a vital man in his late sixties. He reminded me of retired men who've done well for themselves but not grown fat from it. He was calm, articulate and curious. He said he worked in Cornell's geography department, and I sensed goodwill more than judgement in his crisp blue eyes.

'I teach English to migrants,' I told him when he asked.

We were on the little back porch with cups of tea in our hands looking at an unkempt lawn, and he asked thoughtful questions about my job and life back home. I gave a standard answer that teaching your native language was a bit like showing people how to make a cupboard – it was a practical skill, and I mostly liked the relationships with the students. When he asked if I would miss my family, I told him six months wasn't very long.

'America is big,' he said. 'You don't want to travel?'

'I'll get to know it better if I stay in one place,' I said. 'And I've only got the savings to stay somewhere if I rent a room in a house.'

He smiled and nodded, then asked if I had siblings and I told him I had a sister.

'What does she do?' he asked. 'Is she adventurous like you?'

Gnats hovered over the lawn, and it was mid-afternoon. An old bike against a tree in the middle of the lawn was growing long grass through its rusty spokes in the warm still air.

'She's sick,' I said hesitantly.

I realised I couldn't leave it like that without telling him more. I'd learned to avoid talking about Theda with strangers over the years. Aside from them usually not understanding, I was paranoid that my doubts regarding the diagnosis would somehow leak back to my family or the press. It was an unrealistic anxiety, but I felt free of it being so far from Australia. Just being away from that situation made it easier to think.

'It's a physical illness,' I said. 'But there is uncertainty about whether it's also mental.'

He listened well. When I was done, he nodded and told me that his nineteen-year-old son had just died.

'He drowned two months ago,' he said sombrely.

'I'm so sorry,' I said after a beat.

'It was in the lake,' he said. 'Kayaking.'

I nodded and tried to imagine.

'Have you been to Lake Cayuga?' he said. 'It's quite beautiful. It's named after the local First Nations people. It's not dangerous – you could swim across it if you were a good swimmer. It's wide, but a *good* swimmer could cross it.' He paused for a moment. 'My son was a good swimmer. He wasn't great, but he was a good swimmer.'

'Some people drown in the bath,' I said, repeating a cliché my mother had once said when I was young, then I regretted how quickly I'd responded. He nodded and we changed subjects not long after that. The thought of him lingered in my mind after we said goodbye.

★

In the evening, I talked to Patricia about the conversation I'd had with the owner. She was tending something on the stove, and I was sitting on a stool near the spices rack.

'We have a suicide problem in this town,' she said. 'Did he say his son was a high achiever?'

'He said something about him being at Cornell and being well liked.'

'Does that surprise you?' she asked.

'Sort of,' I said. 'I figured … I don't know … at a place like Cornell, life is going well, right?'

'Success doesn't stop people from having mental health issues,' she said, almost sternly. 'You either need to be very smart or have money to be at Cornell. Money will buy you a place. But money and talent don't stop people from being messed up.'

I nodded and tried to imagine the owner's son. Whether he'd drowned intentionally or not was obviously on his father's mind. The family wouldn't get closure. I found I couldn't picture what a life of wealth and achievement looked like – a family of professors and investment properties was an abstract idea to me.

I felt Patricia looking at me, and I realised she was trying to figure something out. She'd noticed the scars on my wrist when we'd had sex the second time. She'd asked about them and I'd talked quite openly. I was used to lovers asking about those scars.

'Ambitious people bring their own kind of baggage,' she said. 'They're generally privileged, that's true. But their sense of self-worth is totally tied up in achievement. Those kinds of families make everything about success. You end up thinking your family won't love you if you don't prove yourself.'

I thought of Rachel. Then I thought of Theda. My mother hadn't pressured Theda or me to be successful. Her love for us kids had always been unconditional. Theda had been neurotic about grades and success anyway. She was proving herself to the world. Maybe, despite her outward rejection of him, she'd always craved our father's approval and knew that academic achievement was something that would get it. I remembered that once, in the early years, before Dad's more committed retreat from parenting, she'd shown him a report card with a litany of A's and he'd chastised her for the one B. But I suspected it was broader than just our father. She had never found a place where she fitted; she was ambitious because success was a way of proving you belonged everywhere.

'Have you ever struggled with depression?' I asked.

'Not really. My mental health has always been pretty good. I see it around me at work, though – more with anxiety, but also some hidden depression. Our department had a suicide a few months ago. I knew the guy. I couldn't tell that he was struggling. He was a bit odd, maybe, but that's not unusual in science. The department offered us all counselling when it happened.'

'Your workplace offered you counselling because someone killed themselves?'

'Of course,' she said. 'It's a university. Universities are good with things like that.'

I could feel myself wanting to scoff. It seemed typical of the highly educated and moneyed to be so precious. I'd watched Theda go through multiple attempts at taking her own life. No one had ever suggested I deserved counselling for it. I didn't know the term *vicarious trauma* and didn't expect help. Seeking help for how someone else's misfortune affected you seemed like an indulgence. But I didn't say anything and would change my mind about that in the coming years.

She went back to stirring and we talked about something else.

After dinner, we had sex again, and I slept over for the first time.

Twenty-Four

In the tenth year of Theda's illness, a doctor suggested she might have chronic Lyme disease. His name was Dr Dixon and he worked out of an integrative-medicine practice in Melville, where my sister was the first patient he diagnosed with the illness. An *acute* version of Lyme disease was a well-known condition and could be confirmed by blood tests. It was curable with a short course of antibiotics. But chronic Lyme disease was difficult to diagnose (it could only be done by clinical diagnosis), and most of the medical establishment dismissed it as unproven. Even among doctors who believed in the diagnosis, there was no agreed-upon treatment for chronic Lyme.

Ticks were understood as the origin of all Lyme disease types; specifically, a bacterium called *Borrelia burgdorferi* carried by them. The theory about chronic Lyme was that if acute Lyme went undetected and untreated, the *Borrelia burgdorferi* would burrow into a person's central nervous system, becoming undetectable, difficult to treat and making the person sick for decades.

The Infectious Diseases Society of America (IDSA) called chronic Lyme disease a myth. Its website warned that the treatments some doctors offered for chronic Lyme disease were dangerous and unproven. It also warned against trusting a couple of rogue medical labs providing 'tests' for chronic Lyme disease. Medical peak bodies called these labs scientifically flawed and unethical. *The New York Times* covered the chronic Lyme lab story in 2005, warning people away from them.

Under the care of Dr Dixon, Mum got my sister's blood sent to one of those labs and the result came back as officially inconclusive, but someone had written on the printout in a thick blue pen next to some odd-looking numbers on the summary page: *Get a clinical diagnosis. This could still be Lyme!*

A clinical diagnosis is when a doctor checks off a certain number of symptoms on a list before giving a name to your illness. Clinical diagnoses are common with mental illnesses, and they apply to some physical illnesses – motor neuron disease, for example.

I saw the list of symptoms used in the clinical diagnosis for chronic Lyme, and I thought it was remarkably long. It was very similar to the symptoms for an M.E. diagnosis. Both of these lists instructed you to check off several symptoms before the diagnostic label could be applied. The symptoms could be intermittent and might change over time. To my eye, the lists were so similar that it was impossible to make a definitive diagnosis without blood tests or scans that might confirm differing causes, and neither diagnosis offered such confirmation.

After giving her a clinical diagnosis, Dr Dixon decided that my sister needed to try one of the experimental treatments that the IDSA had warned against. It was a cocktail of antibiotics administered intravenously on a daily basis for six months. He said that bacteria had burrowed so far into my sister's nervous system that there was no other way of doing it.

It turned out that we couldn't afford the intravenous version of the treatment because you needed a nurse to administer it daily, and Medicare wouldn't pay. So we opted for the oral version.

I remember the first day of this treatment when Mum asked me to come over because it was making Theda vomit and she needed help. My job was to ferry in ice packs and vomit bowls as Mum took the grisly job of picking through Theda's stomach contents with tweezers to identify which pills she needed another dose of. The sheer number of pills she had to swallow was astonishing. I watched Theda taking fistfuls of tablets each time. I'd never witnessed a treatment that made someone so sick.

Mum needed me daily after that, and towards the end of the fourth day everyone's resolve was wavering. Theda was exhausted and couldn't hold up her head. Mum was scared about what was happening. We had six months of this treatment ahead of us and it seemed impossible to get there. Dr Dixon encouraged us over the phone to continue, saying that the vomiting was called the Herxheimer reaction – a phenomenon caused by the die-off of bacteria and fungus in a person's nervous system. We didn't know it at the time, but pumping someone full of antibiotics can also lead to an overdose, and an alternative explanation for the vomiting is just that. Calling such a response the Herxheimer reaction was controversial, and a doctor from the States was on trial for killing a patient, but Mum and Theda trusted Dr Dixon because he was the first person to offer a new ray of hope since the failed Gc-MAF.

Theda's vomiting continued for five more days, and empty pill boxes filled the kitchen bin until the sixth day, when we gave up. After that, my sister fell into a profound depression. She was understandably more exhausted than usual. Her ability to communicate was reduced to a handful of words and glances. She lost all her appetite. Everything she tried to eat brought on waves of nausea, and she couldn't drink liquids without throwing them up. Using a walking frame, she moved from bed to the toilet like a wounded animal.

To keep her alive, Mum started preparing bone broth and providing ice blocks for hydration. It was enough sustenance to live, but my sister's weight looked dangerous. Her joints bulged as her limbs thinned. I could see the skeleton in her face. Her elbows and knees were red and angry-looking around jutting bones. Her skin seemed delicate enough to fall off, parts of it like damp rice paper – once brown, now almost translucent. Mum switched to toddler formula to get Theda the sustenance she could take, but it was a losing battle.

When TV journalists contacted my mother again that year, they wanted to do a follow-up story on the M.E. Mum told them about the Lyme diagnosis, and they said they wanted to do a segment on that instead.

When the story broke, it contained questions for the federal health minister about why his government wasn't doing more to help people like Theda Myint who had chronic Lyme disease. The narrative was that some Perth doctors knew treatments, so why weren't those treatments covered under Medicare? I think my mother believed, possibly correctly, that the intravenous antibiotic treatment wouldn't have been so traumatic.

Pretty soon, new Facebook groups appeared in my life focused on chronic Lyme disease. As with the online M.E. community, I joined out of solidarity but harboured concerns. The groups had the same echo chamber feel, and it was taboo to consider possible causes for the disease that didn't include ticks and bacteria. I noticed many people from the M.E. community were migrating across to the Lyme diagnosis. And I assumed that, like Theda, they'd tried everything for M.E. and not seen improvements, so a new diagnosis offered hope.

Another news channel contacted us, and its media story on Lyme pitted my sister's situation against that of a young woman whom the government had recently given an interest-free loan for a liver transplant. That woman had damaged her first transplant with illicit drug abuse. The question was why that woman was allowed an interest-free loan and not Theda Myint, who wasn't an illicit drug user.

I saw the same pattern of suffering in the online Lyme groups as in the M.E. community. People lived in their bedrooms with parents caring for them as families went bankrupt and broke up under the strain. Patients talked about being ignored and shamed by most doctors. Fathers were often the ones who abandoned parenting in families broken by the stress. Fathers were more likely to tell their children that they didn't believe they were genuinely ill, which made me wonder if something in our culture encouraged men to believe in things only if they could discern a cause, while perhaps women were trained to be more open to uncertainty. Whatever the cause of such things, the outcomes were awful. Suicides were common. Children ended up hating parents who abandoned them.

The chronic Lyme community also had a small branch of extremists. A researcher from Tufts Medical Centre in Boston was being stalked. A journalist had asked this researcher his opinion on chronic Lyme because he had been part of the team who'd discovered acute Lyme disease in the 1980s. He was a target now because he had told the journalist that chronic Lyme was most likely a myth. Since receiving death threats he had had a 24/7 security detail.

I buried my doubts as much as possible for Theda's sake. She constantly asked me if I believed in chronic Lyme disease. It was her new diagnosis and she was probably unsure herself. I always said yes. And in a sense, I was telling the truth. I had once imagined it was a mental illness with physical symptoms, and therefore I'd believed in a mental-illness cure. But I didn't think in such binary terms anymore. I also interpreted her question as being about suffering rather than cause. I didn't blame her and I knew she was suffering, so I gave her the words that meant she knew that.

Pretty soon, Dr Dixon's business was booming as people shared lists of Lyme-literate doctors online just as they had M.E.-literate doctors. Some GPs around the world began identifying themselves as LLMDs – Lyme Literate Medical Doctors. The movement was catching fire but it was a risky move, and Dr Dixon's medical practice kicked him out over the controversy. He believed in chronic Lyme, and it wasn't making him poor, but the consensus in mainstream medicine was that it was unscientific, so he found another building to work in, embraced a marginalised community of patients, and they embraced him back.

I learned something during this time that I never expected. I learned that polarisation can feed on empathy. When we witness suffering, it hurts us too. We look for logical reasons to blame someone or something. It's hard to believe that no one truly understands what's caused the suffering, so we ignore such a possibility and take sides.

In the early 2000s, the attorney-general of Connecticut fought the IDSA over the status of chronic Lyme disease. As the progressive leader of his state, he did so in the name of citizens under his watch with undiagnosed chronic illnesses who were often drawn to the chronic Lyme diagnosis. *Acute* Lyme was prevalent in Connecticut, so chronic Lyme disease seemed a good fit for many people with persistent but unexplained symptoms.

The attorney-general probably wanted to help, but current science and the will of the people were at odds. He joined forces with another senator – Kirsten Gillibrand – who was attempting to sell herself as a progressive after some questionable associations with the National Rifle Association early in her career. Eventually, she would become a self-proclaimed Me Too politician and run in the presidential primaries the year Biden beat Trump. But back in the early 2000s, the two progressives rallied for a moment around people living with medically unexplained illnesses, demanding that chronic Lyme disease be taken more seriously. The peak medical bodies responded that the scientific evidence wasn't there to confirm such a diagnosis.

In the strangest way, I learned more about the psychology of conservatives and progressives by noting how they responded to my sister's illness. Depending on political ilk, anger about suffering was aimed at different targets: Conservatives blamed individuals (patients themselves – lazy and mentally feeble). Progressives blamed institutions and the status quo. Both were capable of being wrong. In the face of uncertainty, partisan politicians took pleasure in expressing the emotional core of their belief systems and arguing logically from there. Political emotions fed the media's hunger to create a spectacle of debate. It snowballed.

In Australia, something unexpected happened. Public debate shifted its focus from whether chronic Lyme disease was an accurate diagnosis to whether Australia had ticks that carried acute Lyme disease. This assumed that the chronic version of the disease was already settled in science, which it wasn't, but I think the press and politicians ran with it because a concrete fight meant everyone could get their emotional fix. Debate over the local presence of those ticks was simpler than an argument over what constitutes a diagnosis. In short, it made for a better spectacle.

At a senatorial enquiry about those ticks, I watched Australian senators become irate as people lined up to tell their stories of heartbreak and despair around chronic Lyme. My mother joined that queue. A few LLMDs like Dr Dixon were there, arguing that the very existence of chronic Lyme patients who had never left Australia proved that Lyme ticks must be in the country. An Australian epidemiologist said Dr Dixon was using anecdotal evidence combined with disproven theories. Dr Dixon fired back. I looked on and asked myself why people weren't arguing more about how to tackle the suffering itself. The grief was palpably present in the room – people there had lost their loved ones. I wondered where it left a society when problems had complicated causes and the solutions weren't necessarily forthcoming. Maybe part of the solution would be to stop seeing a cure as the only thing we need to focus on.

★

As Theda's Lyme disease diagnosis settled in, I noticed a few people in the online forums leaning into conspiracy theories. The main one was that *chronic* Lyme disease had been invented as a biological weapon during the Cold War by the US military on Plum Island, off the coast of Connecticut. Plum Island was near Old Lyme, where acute Lyme disease had been first recognised and got its name. The theory was that the government had taken acute Lyme and weaponised it, which explained why medical professionals were keen to ignore the existence of chronic Lyme – clandestine authorities were paying them off.

Theda didn't fall for this thinking, perhaps because she had once trained as a journalist. She struggled to remember things, and abstract thinking exhausted her, but she still knew how unlikely such a conspiracy was. On the other hand, her need for magical thinking filtered down into her search for treatments. Superstitions and myths grow in desperation, and she purchased a small black piece of plastic online from a company charging almost a hundred dollars for it. Inside were some wires meant to protect the wearer from electromagnetic fields that she'd heard could affect people with chronic Lyme. She also became convinced that household wi-fi was increasing her migraines. She asked our mother to turn it off whenever possible. She asked me to wash my clothes with special detergent and only use non-scented deodorants. I complied, but she didn't notice when I forgot.

Around this time, she developed something called postural orthostatic tachycardia syndrome (POTS). It is a syndrome in which a person's heart rate precipitously rises as they stand. Anorexics and malnourished people often get it. I wondered if it was linked to how rakishly thin she'd become after Dr Dixon's treatment. He assured us the POTS was from the chronic Lyme, and that the ongoing psychotic breaks were also. He said that since we had abandoned the antibiotic treatment, maintaining an even stricter Lyme-friendly diet was the next most important thing. It meant my sister rarely got to eat anything with flavour.

Mostly I didn't feel angry about what was happening, because I knew that we were all up against something no one understood. But sometimes I would feel intense rage at everyone for refusing to see that uncertainty played a much larger part in this situation than anyone was willing to admit.

★

Time is blurry around these events, but I remember meeting Samuel. I cannot remember if he came to us during the M.E. or the Lyme diagnosis, but he was a nutritionist recommended in one of the online forums. He suffered from M.E. and encouraged Theda to take different supplements and adopt a slightly altered dietary strategy. I remember that after her appointment at his practice, which Mum had arranged and executed with the help of a wheelchair, Samuel began visiting Theda at home. He felt a kinship with her suffering and the dismissals she'd gotten from doctors.

When I asked Theda about it, she admitted there was an attraction. 'We often just lie in bed together, Minty,' she said. 'It's so nice.'

Samuel was married but it didn't sound like it was going well. My sister appearing in his life must have felt like a kind of fate, and when his wife left him, he quickly became my sister's boyfriend.

Not long after that, Dr Dixon also diagnosed Samuel with chronic Lyme disease before going on to diagnose himself. In the coming years, an ex-girlfriend of mine would get in touch, saying that she was also under his care. Eventually, many years on, my future counsellor, Eberhardt, would tell me that his wife had received a chronic Lyme disease diagnosis from my sister's doctor.

Twenty-Five

The Airbnb owner emailed me saying I could rent the upstairs room if I signed on for a year. I couldn't stay that long, so he suggested I try a website called Craigslist.

After sending out a few emails, I got a response from a woman named Jane who lived just south of downtown. We made a time and I arrived at her house after lunchtime. It was a big grey double-storey place opposite a used furniture shop.

Jane was a matronly woman in her forties. She told me we were on the black side of town (Jane was white) and that it was good because the rent was cheap and it was a perfectly nice place to live. She explained that two other women were sharing the house with her, and they would be happy to have a man there. The house had a country feel about it. Jane seemed easygoing and said she was local-born – a *townie* – which was unusual for Ithaca.

She took me upstairs to see the room, then we had a cup of tea downstairs in the living room as I casually eyed the thrift-store frames with magazine cut-outs in them – one of Frida Kahlo and another of Van Gogh's *The Starry Night*. The place felt comfortingly like a share house I'd lived in when I was a twenty-something in Melbourne.

She offered me the room after we'd finished our cups of tea, and said the others trusted her judgement enough to let her decide. I appreciated her trust and said I'd gladly take it. She then invited me to a little gathering the household was having the following week to celebrate one of the women getting an article published in a science magazine. 'It'll be a super opportunity for you to meet some people,' she said, beaming.

As I walked back to my Airbnb afterwards, it felt like things were falling into place.

★

Halfway through the following day, Layla Galatas phoned and said she'd spoken to Rachel. Rachel wanted to continue her court action.

'What do you mean?' I asked.

'I mean just that,' she said. 'Rachel said we'd lost her messages. I find it highly improbable. But she accused us of losing numerous phone messages she'd left at our office. That's why she said she'd taken so long to get back to me. I find it very unlikely, though. We have an excellent receptionist.'

'Okay,' I said.

She smacked her lips as if I wasn't grabbing hold of the narrative properly. 'Anyway,' she said, 'you'll have to be here for court on Friday.'

I was in my room and sat down on the bed, nodding to myself. Part of me had assumed Rachel would agree to drop it once she knew I was gone. I couldn't make sense of her wanting me back for court unless she was genuinely afraid of me. That just didn't seem likely, though I supposed it possible.

The air outside my upstairs window was hazy. That haziness always made me feel like I was in a dream. It reminded me of Perth in summer, when smoke drifted down from bushfires in the hills.

'How about the trial?' I asked. 'Did you explain that there is this whole process?'

My lawyer cleared her throat and then explained that there were certain things she couldn't say to opposing party in this situation according to the law.

I wasn't sure what she meant but asked if Rachel knew I had no choice but to fight back.

'I explained that you couldn't simply accept the order of protection,' she said. 'I explained that it affected your future due to your citizenship status. I explained that this would have lifelong consequences for you if you didn't push back against it.'

I could tell by her tone that she wasn't sure she should admit to having said those things to Rachel. I held the phone against one ear. It was enough – Rachel would understand why I was fighting. It still didn't explain why she was fighting *me*, though.

'Rachel was angry, Khin,' she said. 'That was my impression when we spoke.'

'Angry at what?'

'She was angry at me for representing you. She wanted to know how much I was charging. When I didn't tell her, she became threatening. Khin—' She paused and her tone of voice shifted from indignant to questioning: 'Can I ask a question about Rachel?'

'Sure.'

'Is she educated?'

The question surprised me. 'What do you mean by that?'

'I mean does she have a high school diploma or something else?'

'She has a degree,' I said.

Layla Galatas paused. 'What kind?'

'You know – the general type. I'm not sure what you call it here. The type where you study things like anthropology and sociology. She did some gender studies. That sort of thing.'

She smacked her lips again on the other end of the line. 'I would expect anyone with at least a high school diploma to understand something we have in this country called due process. Do you know what that is? I imagine you have something similar in Australia.'

The question was basic. As I began trying to come up with a definition, I felt embarrassed. I hadn't expected fairness when Rachel first accused me. It was the gender politics, which I didn't yet understand, that made me feel that way. Part of me had assumed I was already considered guilty. Perhaps that was because I had spent my whole life in the worlds of women – in my friendships and at work. That was part of what was so uncomfortable about this accusation. It flew in the face of my feeling that I was almost part of the group. I had no community of men around who complained about women. Instead, I had women in my life who often complained about men. They talked about stalkers sometimes, and it had only ever seemed genuine to me. Such men were a dime a dozen. My shame about what was happening now was tied up in that perception. I desperately didn't want to be counted as one of those men.

So, as strange as it sounds to me now, I was embarrassed to think that I would be afforded the presumption of innocence. Being asked to define due process by Layla Galatas drew up that embarrassment again. Sensing my hesitation, she answered for me. She explained some of the basics.

Me Too hadn't yet happened, but it would soon. And I would struggle to make sense of my experiences in that context. Feminism and antiracism are both politics of identity – and I cared about both because gender and race have affected me so powerfully. But I'd also feel stifled when it came time to speak of my experiences because some feminists weren't interested in their complexity. I would eventually come to understand this issue with the help of a metaphor involving a type of Japanese pottery called *kintsugi*. Kintsugi potters smash their work first, then piece it back together using lacquer and gold. The bowls are beautiful and useful, but you can see the cracks where the fragments have been rejoined. The potters argue that to use something well, we must recognise its fragility.

I think of broad social movements like that too now. They are essential and help us understand ourselves and the world. They embody justice and offer us concepts and vocabularies for making sense of our traumas. They provide a field for people to speak when their experiences have been collectively ignored. But pretending they don't have vulnerabilities and exceptions is a fantasy. To use them well, we need to acknowledge their contingency. Not least of all because, down the line, societies reject fantasy. A thing is resilient when we acknowledge its cracks.

On the phone, Layla Galatas explained that Rachel had yelled and eventually hung up on her. 'My guess here is that we are dealing with a certain level of maturity,' she said to sum up. 'It was all very "big American movie". Anyway, make sure you're in Albany for court on Friday.'

★

After the call, I went for a long walk. I passed some large gorges at the edge of town. I thought about how much I adored Rachel. I'd also desperately needed a way out of Perth when we met. Layla's assertion that Rachel was immature only felt right after everything that happened. It wouldn't have earlier. But maybe that was an illusion, and I had chosen someone who couldn't really understand me. I had a lot more life experience than Rachel. I'd never really had enough conflict with her to know how she dealt with life's pressures. It was one thing to see contradictions in other people and quite another to recognise and accept them in yourself. Rachel was excellent at the former, but maybe I should have chosen someone older.

I called Dad when I got back. I explained the situation and said I didn't have money for a trial.

'Son,' he said. 'In life, we create situations that we must take responsibility for.'

I thanked him and hung up.

I knew that I probably needed to call Jane and tell her that I couldn't take the room in her house, but I didn't want to. Maybe I could go hang out in Asia instead? I couldn't reroute my return flight, but maybe I could afford a new one since Asia was so cheap. At least I'd be away from Perth still. I wanted to forget everything and start over somewhere new. Perhaps it was the main reason I was so attached to staying in the US – because I could imagine starting a new life here, in a culture that wasn't drastically different from my own, even if I didn't have the means anymore.

Twenty-Six

In 2011, Theda used her walker to get down the hall and into the kitchen while Mum was at the grocery store. She rifled through drawers for a plastic bag and some elastic bands, then searched for a peaked cap. Next, she went to the laundry and retrieved a bottle of Valium along with two boxes of Tramadol before returning to her bedroom.

She swallowed the pills and tied the bag over her head per instructions in a book she'd read. A peaked cap was meant to keep the bag away from her mouth and nose, preventing choking, but she hadn't been able to find one, and I think it saved her life. Choking induces panic, so it's harder to resist than suffocation.

Mum returned from the shops and found her unconscious with the bag half pulled off.

Theda regained consciousness the next day in the hospital and the doctors said that was remarkable given how many pills she'd swallowed. After monitoring her kidneys for a day or two, they sectioned her into a locked ward because she'd tipped over into psychosis.

I texted Dad in Thailand, asking him to return, but he refused. He attached a PowerPoint presentation about 'suicide watch' aimed at Burmese refugees, but he said it applied to my sister.

★

Theda was sectioned in Alma Street, a locked ward in Fremantle. Her grandiosity was different this time. She clanged and rambled as usual, but instead of mythic stories about curing Theda, she said we needed to kill Theda to rebalance light and darkness in another universe.

The head psychiatrist at Alma Street didn't take a soft line with her chronic Lyme disease. He ignored emails from Dr Dixon asking him to accommodate my sister's dietary needs and implied that her physical illness was conversion disorder.

Mum petitioned the hospital to have Theda released early, which was a ludicrous idea in my opinion. Theda was completely unmanageable at home like this. But Mum was successful, and I spent the next few days helping to contain the situation at their house. Mum knew that both violence and suicide attempts were likely, so she hid the kitchen knives. Theda began going for plastic shopping bags instead. Mum and I were watching her closely, so any suicide attempt with the bags was futile, but in her psychotic state she seemed oblivious to that. We let her have the privacy of her bedroom, but she kept coming out into the kitchen.

I ended up wrestling with her on the kitchen tiles several times to get plastic bags and other implements out of her grip, while our mother yelled like a punter at a sports match from the sidelines.

★

A few days later, Theda apologised. 'I can't believe I act like that, Minty,' she said. 'It's like I have a totally rational reason for it at the time, and I can even remember my reasoning, but it's only after the psychosis that I understand how crazy that reasoning is.'

I told her it wasn't anything to worry about. She talked about how if she did succeed, she hoped there was nothing after death. I listened and then we laughed at something, though I forget what it was.

Four weeks later, she attempted suicide again.

I reached the hospital before the ambulance and waited alongside a man with an oxygen tank. When paramedics pulled my sister from a vehicle, the man with the tank ran over and put a mask over her face before they whisked her through some sliding doors.

I didn't see her again until the evening. She was in Fremantle

Hospital's intensive care unit. A young doctor explained that it was a coma, and although he couldn't guarantee she'd wake up, it seemed likely. He was mainly worried about her waking up with brain damage from oxygen starvation.

When I finally saw her, I touched her hand. Machines were forcing her to breathe. I didn't often cry, but that day the tears came.

★

A couple of days later she woke up psychotic and it was another dark and self-destructive state. They sectioned her in the Alma Street ward again, where the same psychiatrist held the line about refusing Dr Dixon's dietary and supplement treatments.

Dad came back. I had texted him using the words 'coma' and 'brain damage' after crying over my sister in the ICU. It must have hit a nerve.

Theda and Dad hadn't spoken in years, but while psychotic she was unaffected by her usual resentment towards him. He likely couldn't make sense of her pressured and clanging speech but he seemed affected by what he saw. I told him I was glad he'd returned and that the main issue was making sure Mum and Dr Dixon didn't get Theda released before the psychosis wore off this time.

'Hospital is the best place for her, mate,' he said, as if I was opposing such an idea.

'I know that,' I confirmed.

'You think your sister has a physical illness?'

'I don't think it matters,' I said.

'This is the stupid Western thinking, son. You Westerners think the mind and body are separated. Buddhists—'

'I get it,' I said.

He shook his head in annoyance, and I couldn't tell if he was annoyed with me or the situation. I noticed, however, that he was no longer talking as though Theda's problems were purely mental in origin. Instead, he was talking about the mind and body being interlinked and

221

inextricable, which was the non-binary position I'd started coming to more over the years. It wavered sometimes. At times I thought her illness was curable by helping her process repressed developmental traumas; other times I believed it was in her viscera regardless of its origin and that a cure might come from anything.

Either way, I think my father saw me as a parrot of my mother. To him, I would always be too Western. I could explain that we agreed, but the idea couldn't compute because it didn't match how he imagined me. He needed to imagine me that way so he could make sense of himself. It's funny how even people you love can do that.

He stayed a week and then returned to Thailand.

★

Theda was discharged after Dad left.

A reporter supplied Mum with a hidden camera and told her to record the psychiatrist denying chronic Lyme treatments suggested by Dr Dixon. She followed that advice, and the journalist's producer called the hospital director to threaten an exposé about the Alma Street ward's dangerous and unscientific dismissal of chronic Lyme disease. The hospital director instructed the psychiatrist at Alma Street to treat Theda's Lyme or discharge her, so he chose to release her.

Mum needed help getting Theda home. I was conflicted because I didn't agree.

I didn't know it was happening until Mum called. She'd had a spell of vertigo while packing Theda's things. She needed me to take charge of getting my sister and her home.

Someone buzzed me in at Alma Street.

I found my sister's room with the lights off. Theda was pacing against the wall and muttering to herself, while Mum was on the edge of the bed being sick into a kidney-shaped bowl. I knew these vertigos. She'd had them since I was young, and they meant she wouldn't be able to move for a few hours. I saw a half-packed bag on the floor.

Mum couldn't talk because of the vomiting and I realised I had an opportunity to stop Theda being discharged if I was careful.

In the corridor near the plexiglass cubby, I pressed the buzzer and a nurse appeared. I explained that I didn't think Theda could be safely discharged.

'She's still completely psychotic,' I said.

The nurse stammered something about getting the psychiatrist, then vanished behind a closed door at the back of the cubby. A moment later, a slender man in his forties appeared in the corridor and called me over. He was tall, with a neatly scissored dark brown beard, and I recognised him as the head psychiatrist, though we hadn't spoken before.

'You're the brother?' he said officiously.

'Yes,' I said. 'I'm Theda's brother.'

His eyes quickly scanned me. I responded by looking at the most unusual thing about him, which for me was his front shirt pocket. It had a row of coloured pens clipped behind a transparent plastic pocket protector. I had never seen a pocket protector in real life.

'My mother was wrong trying to get her discharged,' I said. 'We can't handle her like this.'

'We have already discharged your sister,' he said.

'She's talking about the need to "kill Theda" and rebalance the forces of light and darkness in another universe,' I said, meeting his gaze.

His voice was neutral but his eyes betrayed contempt. 'Your mother has assured us she can take care of her.'

'Look,' I said. 'I know my mother has caused you trouble. But Mum is doing what another doctor tells her. Theda is dangerous like this. She tried to kill Mum when she was psychotic once. Releasing her isn't a sensible idea.'

'You need to help then,' he said.

'How?'

'First, get them home. Then stay with them.'

'No,' I said firmly. I felt horrid betraying Mum so much. This man was a bastard. But I needed him to agree with me. My betrayal of the family narrative was complete because I was asking him to do the opposite of what I knew Mum wanted. He repeated that Mum could deal with Theda's psychosis at home.

I told him that my sister would jump out of the vehicle if I tried to drive them home.

'Have your mother control her in the back,' he said. 'Take the back roads.'

In coming years, I would hear more about this psychiatrist and his Alma Street psychiatric ward. There would be a Royal Commission inquiry into Alma Street's practices following two murders and two suicides relating to this man's early discharge of patients.

'Mum's had a vertigo,' I said. 'She can't move.'

His face soured and he nodded, more to himself than me. He glanced at the plexiglass cubby. 'Yes,' he said, a cautious tone entering his voice. 'I am aware that your mother has had some kind of episode.' He inhaled and held it for a moment, then said, 'You can have the room until your mother has recovered.'

He tried to leave, but I asked another question. 'Mum needs Stematil,' I said, 'to stop the vomiting.'

He shook his head. 'We can't give your mother medicine.'

'You can call her GP—'

'No,' he said. 'If you're concerned about your mother, you can take her to Emergency.'

'Won't we have to wait there?'

'It depends on how busy they are,' he said.

I asked if there was a way of getting there without using the street. The Emergency Department was two blocks away.

'Not for the public,' he said.

I asked if he could spare a nurse to help me get Mum there in a wheelchair.

'No,' he said. 'You have to excuse me. I have other patients.'

He left and I went back into Theda's room. I tried to talk to Mum but she couldn't properly converse with me. I wanted her to go into the corridor with my help, then vomit on the floor. I was angry. I thought they couldn't ignore that – they'd have to clean it up. It was fine to refuse help if Mum was the only one suffering from her vomiting. They would change their minds once it became their problem too. Mum couldn't speak and didn't budge. When I tried to get her to stand, she shrugged me off.

I returned to the plexiglass cubby and pressed the buzzer several times, but no one came. On my way back to Theda's room, I saw a wheelchair. It had the word *PSYCH* stencilled on its backrest, and they'd obviously left it out for me because it hadn't been there before.

Getting Mum onto the street took about fifteen minutes because she kept needing to stop so she could retch. There were ramps down to the road, but she couldn't hold herself properly in the chair, so I stopped a few times to push her back into it. Once on the sidewalk, the trip to Emergency took another twenty minutes because she couldn't handle me moving her quickly. It was Friday night and I remember the sounds of people calling out to each other in the distance as I held tightly to the wheelchair's handles. The voices sounded drunk and lively, and it seemed strange to me that our different experiences could inhabit the same moment of time.

Twenty-Seven

On Thursday, 25 July, at 7 a.m., I walked down to the bustling little Ithacan coffee shop on the corner of Aurora and Seneca streets, where I'd been having coffee every morning since I'd arrived. It was busy and I ordered, then sat down at a table and waited for my bagel. I flipped open my laptop and double-checked my coach's arrival time. I had the clothes I needed in a gym bag – I was leaving my suitcase there and would spend the night in Albany, appear in court tomorrow morning, then return to Ithaca the day after. I had told Patricia in the end. Keeping my legal troubles secret from her felt wrong since I was leaving town for three days. She would wonder why, and I would either need to lie or come clean. Explaining to someone I was newly involved with that my ex was charging me with stalking felt horrid, but she'd been gracious and said it didn't sound like my fault. I hadn't expected that and was both surprised and relieved.

The little blue-and-white Facebook logo sat at the top of my screen as I scrolled, and I saw that Mum had posted in the online Lyme support groups. She often did that when times were toughest. I saw some people had replied to her, though I didn't see her original post. My bagel arrived so I put the laptop away.

★

When my phone rang, it was just after 7.30 and I was finishing up in the cafe. It was Mum and the first thing she asked was where I was.

'I'm just about to catch the bus,' I said.

There was a short pause, then she said, 'I'm so sorry, Khin. But she's gone.'

I had my bag in my hand and stood up. I told Mum to hold on as I went to the cafe's door. People were coming in and I needed to get outside. I couldn't make sense of my mother's words, though I had a nagging feeling that she was telling me Theda had died.

'She's gone, darling,' Mum said as I pushed my way out. 'We saw a neurologist yesterday. It was our last hope. She was such an arrogant woman. She told Theda there was nothing she could do and it destroyed any hope Theda had left. I woke up this morning and I knew she was dead. I just knew.'

Mum's voice was calm. I knew my mother in tragic situations. I knew her in emergencies. She was always steady. I didn't feel anything like what people say grief is at first. Instead of heaviness, everything inside me was suddenly and inexplicably lighter than air. It was such a strong perception that I felt like I was floating.

'Who's there?' I said.

'Barbara,' she said. 'And the coroner has taken her body away now. When can you get back?'

'I have to go to court,' I said numbly.

I must have started walking towards the coach station, because I remember the diner on State Street and that I saw people sitting in there. The buildings seemed weird and unnecessary, as though humans made them for some petty reason and just got used to being inside them. I stopped at a corner and texted Patricia, asking her to meet me.

When I got to the station, she was standing in a crisp vintage blue dress beside a grey Subaru. I hadn't explained anything in my text. There was worry in her face. I hadn't ever talked about my sister's illness, so I ushered her towards a little bench just beyond where buses dropped people off, and I tried to outline the basic facts. I needed to tell her that my sister was dead. She didn't even know that Theda was sick. I don't know why I needed to tell her anything because I couldn't feel much, but it mattered somehow that I say it.

★

When I called Mum from the coach, she said she'd emailed the Devisons. She wanted them to drop the case against me so I could come home. I knew I would go home either way now. Of course I would go home. Facts were trying to assemble in my head, and I hadn't realised that I would be returning to Perth so soon until I was on the bus. What else did a person do when their sister died?

'Your father is flying back tomorrow,' she said. 'I'm going to get his monk to do a ritual at the house.'

'I need to call the airline,' I said.

'Do that,' she said.

I phoned Layla Galatas, and her reaction felt melodramatic. She quickly became officious, telling me in clear slow words that I needed to call my mother back immediately and ensure she didn't email the Devisons again. She wanted a copy of the email Mum had already sent.

I called Mum back. I asked if she still had people there, making sure she wasn't alone, and she did. I said I would contact the airline as soon as I got to Albany. After the call, I used the coach's onboard wi-fi and my laptop to check the email. Mum's forwarded copy was in my inbox and I could see Rachel's email address along with her parents' email addresses in the metadata. The email itself seemed hauntingly empty. It was just a single line: *Theda took an overdose last night, she is dead. Khin is on his own.*

Twenty-Eight

'It's a miracle,' Mum said. 'It's like the energy from psychosis is here, but she's not loopy. I know it's against Dr Dixon's advice, but yesterday we went for a walk around the block. I figure, why stop her at this stage? It's not like she's getting better.'

'Good,' I said.

I took the next day off work and met them at Coogee Beach. Theda had asked to be taken and for me to come. She wanted to revisit how things had been when we were little children.

It was a Tuesday, mid-morning, and no one was around, and we set up on a rug in some shade below the wooden jetty and ate cheese with crackers. I hadn't seen Theda eating anything tasty in years, and she commented on how nice it was. Then she pointed a frail arm at a yellow pontoon bobbing in the water. 'I want to swim', she said, 'to that thing.'

'I'll make sure she's safe,' I said to Mum. Theda hadn't been swimming in over thirteen years. Her muscle mass was virtually non-existent, but she was determined. Swimming in the ocean was beyond anything I'd expected when Mum had told me on the phone that things were momentarily better.

We walked down the wet part of the sand. Theda held my arm and tiny shells cracked under our toes. Our mother stayed on the rug, reading a crime novel. Once we were close to the pontoon, Theda let go and waded knee-deep. I watched muscle memory kick in as she emerged from a shallow dive into the metronomic front stroke of a child who'd once learned every movement to please an instructor. The difference between us was in that moment. I was a functional but messier

"

swimmer, and she was like a prefect at a swimming academy. Everything about her was so beautifully formed. She had talent.

When we reached the pontoon, we lay on our fronts and cold ocean water seeped down from our bodies into the hot wood.

'We used to do this at the Bentley pools', she said, 'as children.'

'I remember,' I said.

'You wouldn't swim until one day you jumped in. No one even knew you *could* swim. My stubborn little brother.'

We stayed quiet for an indefinite time after that. The water was like someone had scattered diamonds over a clean turquoise surface that was gently moving them around in the sunlight.

'Did Mum tell you', she said, 'about India?' Her voice was tender and ruminative, like someone who has been looking at old photographs of themselves.

'I think you should go,' I said.

'It's for a treatment,' she said.

'I know.'

'India changed you, didn't it?'

'Get out of this fucking country for a while,' I said.

She asked why India had left such an impression and I did my best to explain how seeing so much suffering had helped put Perth into perspective. I couldn't explain why that mattered, but I think she might have understood.

The India treatment was a gift from some New Zealanders who had read about Theda in an old copy of *Who* magazine in Auckland. They had contacted Mum on Facebook and offered to donate the money for Theda to stay at their guru's 'hospital' in Delhi. I could imagine the type. Older white men who were softly spoken and bright-eyed. They would have discovered Eastern religion late in life.

Mum said she wasn't sure about it, and I'd surprised myself by telling her it sounded like a good idea. I didn't believe in any treatments anymore, but something about the idea was right. Mum put it into words when she said this reprieve was likely temporary and Theda would try to commit suicide again if we didn't have something in place for when it ended.

Theda had gone quiet and was looking out at the water. 'You never loved the beach like I did?' she asked then, reaching an arm over the front edge of the pontoon. She shuffled forwards a bit so she could look at her fingertips dangling above the water. 'I mean, you did as a little boy, but not as a teenager.'

'I got to a point where I didn't want to go brown,' I said. 'It was more important.'

'Me too,' she said wistfully.

'Really?'

'Yes. I didn't want to be Asian.'

'It's cool to be ethnic now,' I said.

She sounded surprised. 'How is that?'

'In places like Fremantle, you know? I guess, I mean – I don't know about the rest of Perth.'

'Fucking hippies,' she scoffed.

'Rose used to say hippies needed to go and watch a bunch of crap television instead of travelling in India.'

She laughed. It was a throaty and full-bodied laugh that I hadn't heard in years. 'People are insane, aren't they?'

I saw our mother in the distance, sitting under the jetty. She looked small and content. Theda and I were both average height, but our parents were short. Mum was tiny, five foot two.

'When you're little,' she said, 'you just think everything can work out.'

★

Two weeks later, I moved over to Mum and Theda's house because they had decided to go to India and Mum needed someone to look after the two little dogs. Money was too tight for a kennel. I had offered to take time off and go with them, but she said the best support I could offer was to ask my father if he would help. Dad agreed to pay half the flight and food costs. The New Zealanders weren't covering flights. He would fly from Thailand to meet Mum and Theda in India.

At the Perth airport when I dropped them off, Theda was back in a wheelchair again. Her reprieve from symptoms had only lasted about five days. I was pretty worried about how Mum would cope with the transfers. She had too much luggage. I was pushing it on a trolley as Mum pushed Theda in the chair. We also had two eskies filled with dry ice and Theda's more volatile medicines and supplements that needed to stay cold. I was worried they might get stopped on the Indian side for travelling with a three-month supply of barbiturates. Between the two of us, we barely managed to get her luggage to the check-in counter using a trolley; there was no way Mum would be able to do it while also pushing Theda through the uneven streets of Delhi on a massive reclining wheelchair.

★

Despite my concern, their arrival in Delhi went off without a hitch, and when I spoke to Mum on the phone regularly after that she said things were going well. Dad had met up with them.

A few weeks in, one of the orderlies at the clinic began making sexual advances on Theda, and the treatment wasn't helping, so they moved on.

'I don't expect it to work anyway,' Mum said, 'but she'll kill herself if we come back now. It doesn't matter what Tibetan medicine is like, I'm going up to Dharamshala to try it. Apparently you can see the Dalai Lama's doctor if you go there.'

I'd been to Dharamshala with Rose. I think Mum made her decision partly because she felt she knew it from my descriptions. It was much less hectic than a lot of India. It was a refugee colony and I liked the idea of them going there. At least they'd be safe.

I told her I'd put her in touch with a friend called Gelek, who was a Tibetan refugee with decent English, some Hindi and good ties in the community.

For the first two weeks things were fine, then Dad returned to Thailand. I don't know what went through Theda's head, but she made her third suicide attempt after he was gone.

Mum's voice was steady over the phone as she explained the situation. 'They couldn't deal with her at the Tibetan hospital,' she said. 'So we are at an Indian hospital somewhere down the mountain. She's in a coma, Khin. The hospital is unlike any I've ever seen before. It has a sink in the corner that just empties onto the floor.'

She called back an hour later and explained that there was no change in Theda. The doctors had pumped her stomach, but she wasn't conscious. The hospital didn't have bedsheets or food. 'It doesn't provide medicines,' she said. 'The doctor here writes the names of things in Hindi on little pieces of torn paper and I go into the streets to buy them from vendors.'

I asked if Gelek was helping. She said he was and asked me to stay close to my phone.

Only in India would you find a hospital without medicine. I thought about the fake medicines that I'd encountered on my trip. Life was so cheap there. A Westerner was an easy target too.

She called back an hour later and said the police were harassing her. 'Suicide is illegal here. This little policeman just kept shouting, "Jail! Jail!"'

'Did you pay him?'

'Yes. Gelek speaks Hindi. He told me what to pay and thinks we'll have to pay again when the hospital discharges her. Khin ... she might not make it.'

After the call, I phoned Dad. I knew Gelek had very little power in India. As a refugee, he was a second-class citizen with no right to leave the encampment. He'd taken a risk if he was down the mountain help-ing Mum at the hospital. I'd once seen Indian police beating a Tibetan homeless man in a public square with sticks in broad daylight. I felt deeply grateful that Gelek would risk his own safety to help my mother.

I wanted Dad to go and help them.

'I can't leave here, son,' he said.

'What do you mean?'

'I have been gone for six weeks already. They need me.'

'You're a volunteer,' I said. 'And your daughter is in an Indian hospital.'

'You must convince your mother to return immediately,' he said. 'This could be the international incident.'

I held the receiver slightly away from my ear. He was shouting. I hated it when my father used the word 'mate'. It didn't suit his Burmese accent.

'India is the third-world country, mate,' he said. 'Anything can happen there. I grew up in a third world, mate. You don't know.'

'I know the developing world well enough,' I said, annoyed. 'I think you should go back and help them.'

Dad and I argued. Near the end of the conversation he asked if I thought things couldn't get worse. It was a rhetorical question. 'Your mother and sister are in the hotel room on the fourth floor,' he said. 'Even if she recovers, she will try again, mate. I guarantee it. She has proven this behaviour. The human mind is like – you observe behaviour. What is this … third, fourth time? If she jumps from their hotel window, she could break her neck, mate. She will need the international medical evacuation. There would be the cost. Someone will lose their house. I can't lose my house. Your mother will lose her house.'

I hung up and phoned a friend from Fremantle. She was part of a group of women who'd been my latest attempt at a new circle of friends since my last trip to Asia. I hadn't been keeping up with them much of late. But I'd recently learned that one was the daughter of one of Theda's previous doctors – the doctor who'd misdiagnosed her with multiple chemical sensitivity syndrome when she'd really been addicted to fentanyl. I recalled that friend telling me that her father was also in charge of international medical evacuations to Perth.

I left a message and she texted back half an hour later saying that a medical evacuation from India would probably cost about two hundred thousand dollars. She asked if we had travel insurance, but insurers had refused to cover Theda. After a few more texts, she wished me luck and added that she understood how stressful it must be because her cat had died of cancer only a year earlier. She said people didn't understand how it felt.

★

Mum and Theda returned two months later, both looking like rats who had been saved from drowning. Mum seemed haunted and Theda looked barely alive.

I returned to my share house in Fremantle, and something in me started to lash out. My irritability had often been just under the surface during my years of trying to fit in there, but it became impossible to ignore now. No one in my social setting knew what my family was going through. I had tried with that new group of women, but nothing they had experienced was comparable and they seemed to find the topic confusing and uncomfortable. They preferred talking about how their latest Brazilian lovers had cheated on them and why they hadn't given up on Brazilian lovers quite yet.

One night after a few drinks out, I got home late and found a man I vaguely knew on the couch. He was a normal Freo guy, Melbourne-born but in love with Fremantle's hippy flavours. He was my housemate's friend and had a sort of hybrid bogan–spiritual masculinity about him. In a few years, most of the people I knew then, including this man on my couch and my housemate, would become part of a movement based around a week-long festival in Western Australia called Blazing Swan – a version of Burning Man imported from California by locals. That festival, and its surrounding culture, would become one of the dominant subcultural forces in Fremantle. One of its precepts would be 'radical inclusion', a concept mainly articulated by white people being flamboyant, highly sexualised and drug addled. That day in Fremantle, I had no clear thoughts on the matter. I was just fuming.

'I fucking hate this town,' I spat, sitting down.

'Steady on, mate,' he said.

My housemate was asleep in her room. She sometimes let him sleep on the couch if they had been drinking. His face looked like a block of wood.

When he said something about negativity manifesting more negativity, and that if I didn't like Fremantle I should find somewhere else to live, I responded less than generously. He then reacted badly to my response. I tried semi-backpedalling, alluding to certain 'family troubles', but he was on a roll. I remember shouting at him. I told him to get out of the house. He didn't want to leave. I told him I would physically throw him out. (He was twice my size and could have flattened me.) I was too angry at the world not to do battle with it. I wasn't even angry that our family was struggling; I was white-hot furious that there was no way of talking about it to anyone without blame being cast on my sister, my mother or me.

The following week, I got into another altercation, this time with someone I cared for a little. She was a German backpacker whom I'd briefly dated. We were friends. She was living in Fremantle for the rest of her working holiday visa, working at a small cafe. She was closing it up by herself, and I was waiting for her to finish sweeping outside when she asked about a party I'd gone to the previous weekend. I said it was full of fakers who talked about nothing, and she got annoyed.

'It's called positivity, dude,' she said in her cute German accent. 'You just have to stop thinking all these negative thoughts.'

I was holding a glass of water and threw it to the ground. Glass spewed over the pavement and I began screaming inchoately. I don't remember what I yelled. I couldn't stand it anymore. I was shouting at the invisible wall that seemed to exist between me and everything. Some people walking past stopped to check she wasn't in danger. The incident blew over, but that didn't solve anything. I felt horrible. I couldn't understand what was happening.

★

Surprisingly, it was Dad who saved me. He rang from Thailand in an uncharacteristic show of concern for my wellbeing. 'I'm worried about you, son,' he said. 'You should leave for a while. We have refugees here who need English teachers – can you come?'

He sweetened the idea by explaining that it wouldn't cost me anything more than the flights because he could arrange a USAID stipend. He said there were lots of intelligent and attractive young Western women who worked with the Burmese refugees.

I remember thinking that young people with political passions aimed at refugees might be more amenable to a less sunshine-and-rainbows world view.

When I asked Mum what she thought, she said she was relieved. She told me to go for as long as I could.

I got on well with my boss at the refugee school in Perth, so I asked for unpaid leave and went. The Thai–Burmese border was destitute. It was dirty and poor and full of problems. But it was healing to be there. I got a position trying to sort out the English language program at an orphan school. English was important for them because without it they had no access to textbooks that weren't filled with military propaganda. I spent ten months trying to sort out their way of teaching English with hardly any materials and with traumatised, uneducated teachers.

One night, I met an American aid worker called Rachel. She was only twenty-four and had bright clear-brown eyes and a body like a reed. She showed a clear and direct interest in me. We slept together and then took regular six-hour trips on dirt roads to see each other for the following months. She usually worked in another town, so it was pure luck that we'd met. As I got to know her, I realised that she was very sharp. She was intelligent and driven. She wanted to do something meaningful with her life that wasn't focused on money. She cared about refugees and poverty. She looked like Anne Hathaway and said she found guys her own age boring. I could barely believe it when she said she was falling in love with me.

She wanted to go to Australia for a while, and if things worked out we'd move back to the States. For the first time in my life, I felt proud of where I was from. I showed her the beaches and the dolphins that swam in the river. I knew there was no future for me in Perth and sharing it with Rachel felt like a last hurrah. She was fascinating, inspiring and brilliant. I realised I would leave Mum and Theda for her. She seemed to come from a luckier life than mine. Her story was plainer and more normal – nothing had gone too far off course. She wanted to change the world, but she also wanted a family, and she was young enough for that not to be a pressure on the present. I wanted to be a part of that future.

Twenty-Nine

The courthouse was stately. Inside was a large space beyond some security checks, and after I got patted down for weapons, I found my courtroom on the third floor. A young-looking black family was waiting with two kids on a wooden pew. The pews were three rows deep, facing the closed door with a sign saying it was Court 6.

Mum had called earlier, wishing me luck. Layla Galatas had emailed that she would call ahead and potentially come late if the court was behind schedule. She said it would save me money because her presence cost five hundred dollars per hour regardless of whether she was in front of the judge or waiting.

She arrived half an hour after me, after the black family had gone in, wearing the same red skirt-suit she'd been wearing when we'd met a month earlier.

'The judge will understand if you need to return for your sister's funeral,' she said, sitting down. 'It's a criminal offence not to appear, but he will understand if you have to postpone. First, I'll need to check what database you're on and whether you'll be allowed back into the country if you leave.'

The idea of a required court appearance and being refused entry to the country made as much sense as anything had. I nodded and figured I'd think about it later. I didn't have the money for leaving and returning anyway. And none of it mattered anymore.

She gave me a pointed look. 'Rachel can stop proceedings at any time until she goes into the courtroom,' she said. 'She could call ahead and let them know it's off. That's up to her.'

Fifteen minutes later, Rachel appeared, looking smart and proud. She didn't look at me. She had a friend in tow whom I recognised from Skype calls made from our apartment in Perth. Rachel was in the same dress she'd worn to my birthday dinner at a fancy restaurant last year, and the friend was similarly elegant. The hem of Rachel's dress was weighted and frilled gently just below the knee.

I'd expected to see her mother, but there was also a certain logic to Mary Devison's absence. Mary's projection onto Rachel was to make her a leader, not a dependent. Her mother was trying to shape her into something formidable, and independence and righteous anger were part of that assemblage. An accompanying parent wasn't the right look or lesson.

As both young women got closer, I stole another glance. Layla and I were a row back from the front. Both women had narrow, delicate faces and whip-like figures. The friend had long, tightly curled blonde hair down to her mid-back, and Rachel's was the same natural light brown as always and almost reached her lower back.

Layla Galatas tapped me on the shoulder. 'Which one is Rachel?'

'Brown hair,' I said quietly. They passed in front of us, porcelain skin and the smell of perfume. I knew that the woman with her was from her church – United Unitarians, a contemporary American phenomenon aimed at young progressives of all faiths. Rachel had talked about it a lot.

The wooden pews had two aisles, so Rachel and her friend could sit pretty far away, and they took the seats furthest from Layla and me.

My lawyer then did something distinct and almost predatory that made me slightly uncomfortable. She shifted in her seat to stare at Rachel for about thirty seconds. It felt designed to intimidate, though she might have simply been trying to understand Rachel's character by watching her in person for the first time for a few moments – I wasn't sure.

After that, we waited for three hours. The pews filled up and I chatted with Layla to pass the time. I didn't know what else to do. I still felt numb about Theda. I couldn't believe it had happened. I asked Layla about her job mostly.

'I don't think I can stay in family law,' she said at one point. 'My boyfriend is a maths teacher in Connecticut. I'll probably move out there and shift to a different type of practice.'

'Why don't you like family law?'

She twisted her lips into a sideways comma and said, 'I don't mind some things about it. I like figuring out complex asset divisions between people who've shared a business. It's technical and satisfying. But people can be so cruel in this type of situation. They use their children to hurt each other. That's the thing I hate the most. It's not about the children's wellbeing – they just want to hurt their ex as much as possible. I don't like being part of that.'

I wondered if perhaps I'd misunderstood her earlier in the week when she'd said Rachel wanted to inflict damage on me. I'd interpreted it as implying something about me and I might have done something to deserve it. I was acutely aware that I was paying her so she wouldn't tell me, but I'd wondered several times in the last month if she privately didn't believe I was telling the whole truth. Now I wondered if people hurting people they had once loved was normal in her world – and if it was, how that changed the way you looked at people and yourself. Anger was a way people made sense of things. Shame was another. Maybe the two were even related.

★

The courtroom was bright and much too large for us. The judge's bench was high and panelled, overlooking us from a distance. The judge wore a black robe and read his papers without looking up as the clerk who'd brought us in fiddled with a recording machine. The Stars and Stripes hung motionless on a short pole. A coat of arms was on the wall with its eagle eye staring, an olive branch in one claw and spears in the other. Obama watched from a portrait, and I recalled seeing a similar one at a train station. Only in that photo he was smiling. It was otherwise identical, taken against the same background, with him in the same suit. I imagined a photographer asking him to do several different expressions in one sitting, knowing that the portraits had different purposes depending on where they ended up. It was absurd how much Americans celebrated their presidents. I couldn't imagine a portrait of the prime minister at a train station in Australia.

When we were all seated, the judge's first act was to ask that we confirm our names, and then he read Rachel's statement aloud. I knew it by heart, and I got the impression he was reminding himself of its contents.

'Yes, judge,' Layla Galatas said when he asked her a question. It was something about whether our party had tried to negotiate. She explained that Rachel hadn't wanted to compromise, but she didn't use the word 'compromise'. She said something more official and bland. She then used a legal term I didn't know – *prima facie* – concerning the charge itself.

'He's not even here anymore,' she concluded. 'He's in *Ithaca*, judge. He caught a bus here today to appear in court and is leaving again tomorrow. This whole proceeding is just because he didn't leave Albany *quickly* enough for the petitioner. She invited him here, Judge. He quit his job and gave up an apartment. She then changed her mind and told him not to come. Judge, he already had the ticket. He came and asked her to meet. She agreed to meet at a cafe, just as she writes in her statement. They met. He agreed the relationship was over and said he wouldn't contact her. He was only in Albany for a few days, Judge.'

'What do you mean "she invited him"?' the judge asked.

I was focusing on details. None of the facts were new to me, so I was curious about how my lawyer had used the word *judge* and how he interrupted her once he'd heard enough. I'd expected her to say *your honour* and wondered if there were many titles you could use in a courtroom for the person deciding everyone's fate. Layla had told me that Rachel would have spoken to him directly when applying for her petition. I had to admire Rachel's confidence. I would have found a judge very intimidating to seek out and speak with. I could hear from his voice that he didn't know the missing details my lawyer was telling him.

Rachel was the next person to speak after the judge asked her to respond. I watched her across the aisle like I was witnessing a medical procedure. I still loved Rachel. I was starting to dissociate the person I loved from the woman I could see now, but it wasn't absolute. She was the only person I had ever thought about marrying. I was thirty-five and I'd never wanted to marry until meeting her. She was special. This event felt like a piece of theatre – from the symbols in the courtroom to the judge's gown and the formality of everything said. It was like we knew it was artificial, but we were playing roles assigned to us by some higher force. We were going through the motions, each of us a fleshy creature with uncertain thoughts, and yet this courtroom and its proceedings demanded we suspend that knowledge about ourselves and pretend.

In this detached mindset, I weirdly thought of mangos. Last year in November, at the start of Perth's summer, mango season began and my boss from the refugee school had given me ten in a cardboard box as a gift on the same night Rachel had worn that dress. We'd both laughed about it later. Richard – my boss – was a funny, somewhat needy man. Rachel and I would ponder him sometimes. His gift was audacious, but we weren't sure if he'd meant it to be. We'd eaten one mango, then tried to freeze the rest. It hadn't worked as expected. When they came out of the freezer and thawed, they were nothing but mush. The freeze had disassembled their cellular integrity and we didn't eat the rest.

Rachel's voice was crisp. 'Your honour,' she said, 'I'd like to say that he didn't leave Albany until the order of protection was served.'

I found nothing odd about this. But it turned out that it wasn't what the judge wanted to know. He asked her if I'd contacted her since the order was served.

'His mother contacted my mother yesterday,' she said.

'Who tried to contact you?' the judge said.

'His mother emailed my mother yesterday.'

'I'm not interested in whose mother emailed who. I want to know if he has contacted you since the order or protection was served.'

I heard an inflection of annoyance in his voice and realised he was irritated at Rachel. I wouldn't understand until later that the missing things in Rachel's statement didn't reflect well on her. He wanted to know if my lawyer's facts were correct, and when Rachel didn't contest them it made her look manipulative. I still didn't know if leaving out facts was considered lying or normal in legal battles.

When Rachel referred to the email again, Layla Galatas was already standing. I didn't notice her get up, and her voice flowed across the room like an electric current. Rachel looked confused by the interruption. Like me, she probably didn't know that interrupting was something a person could do in a situation like this. Her family friend who was a lawyer had turned out to be a bankruptcy lawyer (Layla had looked him up), so Rachel was representing herself. She was doing a better job than I would have. I would have been too intimidated to speak in the tone she was using.

'Miss Devison,' Layla Galatas said. 'I want you to tell the judge what was in that email.'

Rachel was stunned for a moment. She looked at the judge as if to ask whether she was required to answer the question. I didn't see his face, because I was watching Rachel, but no one said anything for a second or two.

'His sister died,' she said. 'But—'

The judge interrupted her before she finished. He'd had enough of manipulated facts and half-truths. He spoke to Rachel fairly, but it was clear he wasn't sympathetic. He was more sympathetic to me. I hadn't spoken except to say my name, but he said something about not contacting Rachel again if I wanted an easy life. Then he dismissed the case. Maybe the look on my face said something to him in combination with finding out my sister had just died. I'm not sure.

Since arriving in America, I'd had an opposite experience to Rachel in many ways. America was new and exciting. It didn't make me feel

I should be doing more with my life. In fact, it was a relief from the questions I had back home about whether I could continue living in Perth for Mum and Theda, and whether I was supposed to save my sister's life by getting that drug away from her. I was still confused about whether I or anyone else really understood Theda's illness and whether that meant some treatments remained untried. I wasn't confident I could face becoming Theda's carer one day if she outlived Mum. And I was uncertain about Rachel's leaving too – her real reasons, why the sudden doubt – and whether her imploring me to be a 'fucking man' and wanting someone bolder and rougher meant I'd misunderstood what intelligent, progressive women wanted from their partners or whether Rachel was just toying with those things as she figured herself out.

The only thing I knew for sure that month was that coming to the United States would show me something. It would show me whether or not I could save my relationship. I'd never had a plan beyond arriving. When Rachel wasn't keen on salvaging things, I'd stayed because it was a holding pattern. I could pretend back home didn't exist in a way. I didn't need to face it and everything it meant. I had reached the cumulative load of ambiguity in my life and I needed some space to think. I'd wanted to feel dislocated and distracted.

★

I walked out of the courtroom. The time in front of the judge had been fifteen minutes. Rachel was rushing and Layla Galatas was shouting something at her back. I felt uncomfortable about that, too, like in the waiting room when my lawyer had stared at her.

'Miss Devison,' she called out, 'don't try to contact my client!'

Once outside the courthouse, she said, 'Don't respond if she contacts you. She's been humiliated. I can imagine a scenario where she tries to draw you into some kind of dialogue about your sister to try and drag us back to court again, saying you've been in contact.'

I thought it improbable. Rachel wasn't a bad person. And yet I could feel something in me shifting. My sense of people was somehow 'off'. I had deeply trusted someone who'd treated me in ways I never could have predicted or imagined.

I read later that betrayals can be among the most troubling experiences because they disorientate us. They echo forwards in our lives and the choices we make. I would lose direction in the coming months and years. I would be doing something and suddenly become frozen. It happened in shopping centres at first, then in other settings. I would be looking at the cereal boxes and suddenly be filled with a mixture of anxiety and anger. That rage would be mixed with feelings of grief for a world I had imagined existed before these events, and an uncertainty about what world was supposed to replace it. Those powerful emotions wouldn't emerge for a while, but when they did it would feel like a loss of innocence. My way of coping during these events hadn't included anger. But afterwards anger would come, and I wouldn't know where to put it, or even what it meant. I would eventually see how it related to feeling profoundly disorientated.

The instincts we rely on to guide us through the world are fragile. They are fallible but necessary. It's a contradiction – we have to rely on them, yet they will never be reliable. Mostly we can live with that, but sometimes it gets too much when the stakes are high, when we feel we've lost too much, damaged ourselves or others, or been horribly misunderstood. If our instincts led to such things, accepting how fallible our intuition is gets too hard. Our whole selves can crumble. It can make the future impossible to imagine. We need faith; at the same time we need to understand that it is an illusion.

Many years later, I would be walking in the streets of Tokyo, listening to a lecture that I'd downloaded from the internet about some philosopher who proposed that seeking orientation was our fundamental human urge. It was at a time when the world seemed to be in the throes of polarisation, driven by the flood of too much contradictory information. Trump was in the White House, social media was a dumpster fire and I was desperately trying to heal something that still wasn't well inside of me.

I would begin reading about disorientation after that, trying to understand what had happened in me and how I might heal it. I would learn about the psychology of ambiguity, about our tolerance for it, and read Jorge Luis Borges's story about a civilisation that tried to eradicate uncertainty by making a map of the world as large as the world itself. But an Italian philosopher named Luciano Floridi would be the one to put it most succinctly for me. He wrote that uncertainty is like cholesterol: too much can kill, but a total absence is also bad for us. How to live with it remains elusive when making a wrong move can destroy everything we care about.

I remember the growl of Layla Galatas's two-seater sports car. It idled in the driveway of my B & B while I fumbled with the door code. I could feel her eyes on me. Now that her job was done, I imagined she was wondering who I was. I had a moment of paranoia that she might imagine I'd lied about staying here and was only pretending to open the door when my real plan was to head off to Rachel's house and harass her some more.

Once I got inside, I breathed a sigh of relief.

Up in my room, I called Mum.

Thirty

Perth was rainy, and Mum drove us from the airport to her house amid gusts of wind. I'd felt sorrow about leaving America. My last night before flying back had been spent in Brooklyn at a hostel. The US was hostile to an easy life in so many ways, but as I'd viewed Brooklyn from a rooftop I had reflected on how many different kinds of people lived there. Rachel was right in imagining that I would be attracted to her country. I didn't know how Perth would be now that Theda was gone. Maybe easier. But despite its unfamiliarity, America had felt a lot like home.

'Your father has been rifling through her room,' Mum complained as she drove. 'I've got him staying in the spare room. You'll be in my room, and I'm in Theda's. But when I'm out of it he's been going in there and finding things he wants to take. They're not even sentimental things. That would make sense – they're all that technology and stuff he likes. He asked if he could have her iPod and some of her electrical cables.'

I wound down the window and smelled the air. The scent of eucalyptus trees getting wet reminded me where I was.

When we reached her house, Dad was subdued. He'd hurt his back on the plane and was resting it. That evening we all watched *The Best Exotic Marigold Hotel* together and didn't talk much.

★

The next day I noticed some things about my parents. Mum wasn't crying. Dad spent most of his time at the desk in the spare room on his computer. He left the door open in the afternoon, and I saw some items on the mattress. There were two tennis balls that I assumed he was using for back stretches. And my sister's vibrator.

Theda had always been candid with me. Once, when she'd been recovering from a psychosis, she was still in a locked ward and asked me to make sure her vibrator wasn't out from under her bed, because she knew she'd made a mess of her bedroom. She said Mum would tidy it up before she was released and she didn't want her finding it. I knew what it looked like because of that.

Now it was on my father's mattress.

'Are you using Theda's vibrator as a back massager?' I said to him.

He looked up from his computer. 'This is just an object, mate,' he said.

'She wouldn't have liked it.'

He screwed up his face. 'This is Western bullshit. You Westerners are so attached to symbols. Buddha didn't even want representations of himself, mate. It was the bloody Westerners—'

'She wouldn't have liked it,' I repeated, knowing where my father was going. His anger at how the West had commercialised and appropriated Buddhism cut into his sense of self.

'She is gone, mate,' he said defiantly. 'Mind and body are interdependent. This is the fundamental Buddhist teaching that Westerners do not see about Buddhism – Pratītyasamutpāda – interdependent co-arising: body, sensation, perception—'

'She wouldn't like it,' I repeated.

'You are like Thai businessmen,' he said. 'On the border they are just like the Westerners. They have been corrupted by the Western thinking. Ex-prostitutes, mate – Burmese refugee women set up the laundry business to have a better life. These were the refugee women, mate – exploited victims. But Thai businessmen wouldn't use it. They said that those women were "symbolically" dirty. This is the stupid Western—'

'Why don't you ask Mum?' I said, pushing the point.

He straightened his back, and I realised I'd made a mistake. He would ask her, and she'd be upset. Insecure men were so predictable. Their need to be right was really about a low sense of self-worth and fending off imagined attacks to their core. It was obstinate and impoverished at the same time. But it hurt people with its blindness.

I abandoned the argument, feeling guilty. He was jealous of me and I knew it. Anything I threw at him became a competition. He was jealous of my mother's approval of me too. Drawing her in was a stupid move on my part. It was so strange how shame worked. Denied, it found a way to rule you somehow. Weird knots of shame were twisted around an Asian man's masculinity complex in the West. Asian men were emasculated here. I had seen it in high school, but the Asian boys had congregated with each other and ignored it. Dad's problem was that he'd tried to mostly move in a white world without a Burmese community.

These were typical thoughts I had about my father whenever we argued. I needed them to accept who he was without being hurt or cutting him out as Theda had.

★

The house was silent until five o'clock. When Mum knocked on my door, she said we were going to the funeral parlour. We drove together and Dad took a car he'd borrowed from someone else.

'He put it back,' Mum said, when I asked about the vibrator. 'He wasn't like that before, you know.'

'I know,' I said.

'I don't know what makes people change.'

When we got to the funeral home, Mum's phone started dinging.

'It's Dr Dixon,' she said. 'He thinks I've chosen the wrong lab for Theda's brain.'

'Her brain?'

'I've had it sent to a Lyme research lab over east.'

'Ignore it,' I said. 'He doesn't matter anymore.'

She nodded distractedly and fiddled with her phone as we crossed the car park.

'It's not going to make a difference,' I said.

'She would want her death to help other people,' she said.

'We did everything we could.'

She still looked worried but nodded and turned her phone off before we stepped inside the viewing room.

When I entered, a mood came over me and I was suddenly afraid. A coffin was against the back wall. Staff had put lights above it and surrounded it with flowers. The design of the box was cheesy and cheap-looking, with black musical notes painted on its white surface. My sister's body was inside. A thought flashed into my head that as with everything to do with Theda's life and death, Mum had needed to make the arrangements for the funeral. It wasn't a bad choice. It was cheesy in a way Theda would have liked.

As I walked towards Theda, I was aware of Mum hanging back a bit and Dad edging around the side of the room. I went slowly down the middle and met the body sooner than everyone else. My reaction when I saw her was unexpectedly doubtful. Her fingertips seemed too thin at the ends. It was like a skilled doll maker had made a replica and got the fingers slightly wrong. Her face wasn't the right shape, either.

Dad was playing with a latch near the top end of the coffin, saying something about how it must keep the lid closed when the time came.

When I touched Theda's hands, they felt stiffer than I'd expected and completely cold.

Dad moved around to the next latch and fiddled with it, saying the same thing about its mechanism, as if confirming this to himself. After that, I moved out of the way so he could get closer to the body. He touched her hands, which silenced him.

My mother suggested I have some time by myself in the room. She led my father out and left me alone.

Once it was just the two of us, I wept uncontrollably. I sobbed, with words tumbling out that made no real sense. I promised I would be 'good' over and over.

★

On the drive home, Mum said my father had started opening drawers and cupboards in the parlour foyer and commenting on all the documents he found inside. She said a woman had come over to ask if everything was okay, and he'd tried to joke with her in an almost flirty way.

'You know how he gets around white women,' she said.

I tried to remember if he was the same way around Burmese women. He only started acting erratically when he was unsure of himself.

The next day, I asked him if we could go for a walk. We sat down at some tables in a local supermarket cafe and I told him that if there was anything he was feeling, he should share it.

'I'm fine,' he said.

'Don't you think it's coming?'

'What?'

'Feelings of grief.'

He looked annoyed. 'Buddhism taught me non-attachment,' he said. 'I'm pretty sure I'll be fine.'

★

It was sunny and cool on the day of the funeral. We drove to Cottesloe Beach with Theda's ashes. Samuel and his family joined us. My Burmese cousin and some locals from the online Lyme community came.

When we arrived, I saw a woman in a wheelchair I recognised from the online Lyme groups. She was one of Dr Dixon's patients. She looked about twenty and was rake-thin. She recognised me, gripped my hand, and told me that Theda was her hero.

After that, we walked down to a rocky jetty. We walked out on it until the ocean was on either side of us. My Burmese cousin tried to speak to me. 'I miss Theda ... Feeling bad for Theda,' he said.

We formed a circle, and everyone took turns talking. Mum and I weren't planners, so neither of us had come up with a speech.

'She asked permission,' I said when it was my turn. 'Mum and I both said yes. It meant she didn't feel guilty.'

When Dad spoke, he looked embarrassed and sad.

The group passed around the urn as I climbed down to the water, and my cousin crouched on the rock above mine to pass it to me. He smiled like the Rangoon sun. Ships sat on the horizon, and I emptied the ashes as people tossed flowers over my head.

As we walked back towards the car park, I saw my father walking alone and quickened to join him. I put an arm around his shoulders. Mum was nearby and came to my other side. I put my free arm around her. And the three of us walked like that – two short parents and their remaining tall kid – and I thought about everything we'd done to each other, about how uncertain life was. I thought about fragile creatures.

Acknowledgements

Generous people helped me find my way as I wrote this. Ella Cross, you nurtured me through some of my darkest moods as I wrote and grieved. Without you I wouldn't have been okay. David Whish-Wilson, your principled and generous advice was invaluable. I was lucky to meet you. Thor Kerr, thank you for guiding me toward good cultural thinkers. Dad, I remember watching you change in the decade after Theda died. Especially in the months before you passed away, I connected with the beautiful man inside you. Thank you for telling me to write this as I saw it, not as you might have hoped I did. I love you. Theda, my closest friend, I miss you. Kristina Olsson, thank you for being a careful mentor. Veronica Sullivan, seeking a publisher without you would have overwhelmed me. You and the Wheeler Centre's Next Chapter played a key role in this book's existence. Chris Feik, thank you for believing in this story and my way of telling it. Kate Hatch, your attention to detail has been invaluable. Julienne van Loon, I suspect you helped me more than I know, both with advice and opportunities. Olga Lorenzo, our friendship gave me confidence. You helped me face emotions I shied away from. You're missed. Liz Byrski, thank you for reading my manuscript and encouraging this project. Tim Loveday, I hope we have many more memories to make as friends and allies. Kate Davis, you helped me think. Amy Cowan, you and your family are remarkable. Ruth, you bring me continuous joy. You love and accept me with your whole heart. How lucky I am. Lastly, Mum: you raised Theda and me with too little help. When people spoke down to you or abandoned you during your hardest times, I wonder if you realised that your compassion was much more significant than their thoughts and actions. Privilege and tertiary education don't come close to your humane and intuitive way of moving through the world, blessing the people you care about. You let me write this how I felt, which wouldn't have been easy. More than that, you taught me the most significant lessons: to be kind and adventurous.